LOST AIRLINE COLOURS OF ASIA

This book is for everyone who has ever suffered as a result of an airline failure, whether staff or passenger. It might be a look back at what was, but I would also like it to be about hope for the future, with new entrants looking to succeed in the void left in this fascinating industry. As this book is being written during the first lockdown of 2020, I am well aware that there may well be a great deal more airline colours lost by the time you get to read this.

First Edition 2021

ISBN 978 1 8380086 3 5

The information in this book is true and complete to the best of our knowledge. All recommendations are made without any guarantee on the part of the Publisher, who also disclaims any liability incurred in connection with the use of specific details or content within this book.

All rights reserved. No part of this book may be reproduced or transmitted in any form or by any means, electronic or mechanical, including photo-copying, scanning, recording or by any information storage and retrieval system, without permission from the Publisher in writing.

© 2021 Martyn Cartledge

British Library Cataloguing-in-Publication Data
A catalogue record for this book is available from the British Library.

Published by Destinworld Publishing Ltd.
www.destinworld.com

Cover design by John Wright

PREFACE

Martyn Cartledge

The airline business has always been a difficult game to play, with many a good idea never reaching its full potential and falling by the wayside, be it through management failures, political machinations or underhand corporate dealings.

The business has also always been particularly vulnerable, often becoming a physical target for terrorist groups wanting to further their cause. Or when it comes to major incidents triggering reductions in demand for, or the ability to, provide air travel. SARS, Ash clouds and perhaps the biggest so far – the Covid-19 pandemic. It is perhaps a little ironic that this latter crisis is what has given me the time to write this book whilst all the time knowing that with 90% of the world's airline fleets sat in neat rows on the ground, there will unfortunately be a number of other possible entries that could have been included once the dust settles and government aid ceases, if it was ever there in the first place!

However, this industry also has a habit of bouncing back. Some airlines will be lost of course, some will rebrand and rise from the ashes to fight again, but others will have been more prepared and will take the opportunity to trim operations and hopefully become a leaner, more efficient outfit once they can return to more normal operations, albeit at the horrendous cost to their, now redundant, employees.

This book is all about what has gone before, be it a change of livery for a currently operating airline or to remind us of the airlines that are no longer with us, as well as the odd special livery once advertising a long since passed event.

The book is separated into the countries that are considered by the United Nations to be in Asia. I have to confess that there were a couple of surprising entries, most notably Cyprus which is so culturally and politically European that I never even considered it as a possibility. As such, rightly or wrongly, I have decided not to include any airlines from there. Turkey is a country that sits on both continents, and with so many defunct airlines, you will see entries included, as there are enough to be in books about both Asia and Europe.

Even though I consider myself pretty good at geography of the world, if you had asked me about Israel and on which continent it sat before researching this book, I think I would have struggled. I have tried to include at least two airlines from each country, but this has not always been possible due to a number of reasons. So please forgive me for this, and if I have not included your favourite, there are simply far too many to include them all.

All the photos are mine unless otherwise credited, and to those people who filled the gaps in my collection, I am very grateful.

This is my second book, but the excitement, and indeed frustrations, of its creation and the anticipation of its eventual publication are just as great as with my first, Flying Firsts. I hope you enjoy reading it as much as I did creating it.

LIST OF COUNTRIES (INCLUDING DEPENDANCIES) IN ASIA ACCORDING TO THE UNITED NATIONS

Afghanistan	7	Maldives	67		
Armenia	9	Mongolia	68		
Azerbaijan	11	Myanmar	69		
Bahrain	12	Nepal	70		
Bangladesh	15	North Korea	72		
Bhutan	17	Oman	73		
Brunei	18	Pakistan	75		
Cambodia	19	Philippines	79		
China	21	Qatar	81		
Georgia	28	Saudi Arabia	83		
Hong Kong	29	Singapore	85		
India	35	South Korea	87		
Indonesia	38	Sri Lanka	89		
Iran	42	State Of Palestine	90		
Iraq	45	Syria	91		
Israel	47	Taiwan	92		
Japan	51	Tajikistan	96		
Jordan	54	Thailand	97		
Kazakhstan	56	Timor-Leste (East Timor)	101		
Kuwait	57	Turkey	102		
Kyrgyzstan	59	Turkmenistan	105		
Laos	60	United Arab Emirates (UAE)	106		
Lebanon	61	Uzbekistan	108		
Macau	64	Vietnam	109		
Malaysia	65	Yemen	111		

Lost Airline Colours of Asia

ALPHABETICAL LIST OF AIRLINES

Air ACT	102	Etihad	106
Air Alfa	103	EVA Air	93
Air Astana	56	Fly Georgia	28
Air China	22	Flynas	84
Air Hong Kong	29	FlyVista	28
Air India	35	Garuda Indonesia	38
Air Koryo	72	Great Wall Airlines	26
Air Kyrgyzstan	59	Gulf Air	12
Air Maldives	67	Hong Kong Express	34
Air Mekong	109	Iran Air	42
Alyemda	111	Iran Aseman Airlines	43
Amakusa Airlines	51	Iraqi Airways	45
Ariana Afghan Airlines	7	Japan Airlines	51
Arkia	47	Jeju Air	88
Armavia	10	Jet Airways	36
Armenian Airlines	9	Jett8 Airlines	85
Asia Atlantic Airlines	97	Kampuchea Airlines	19
AtlasGlobal	103	Kingfisher Airlines	37
Azerbaijan Airlines	11	Kish Airlines	44
Biman Bangladesh Airlines	15	Korean Air	87
Business Air	97	Kuwait Airways	57
CAAC	21	Lao Central Airlines	60
CargOman	74	Malaysia Airlines	65
Cathay Pacific	30	Mandarin Airlines	94
Cebu Pacific	79	MAOF	49
China Airlines	92	Merpati Nusantara Airlines	39
China Eastern Airlines	22	MIAT	68
China Express Airlines	25	Middle East Airlines (MEA)	61
China Northern Airlines	23	Myanmar Airways International	69
China Northwest Airlines	24	Nippon Cargo Airlines	52
China Southern Airlines	25	NokScoot	100
China Southwest Airlines	25	Oman Air	73
Dragonair	31	One-Two-Go	98
Drukair	17	Pakistan International Airlines (PIA)	75
El Al	48	Palestinian	90

Philippine Airlines	80	Tajik Air	96
Qatar Airways	81	Thai Airways International	99
Royal Brunei Airlines	18	Tigerair Mandala	41
Royal Jordanian	54	TMA	63
Royal Nepal Airlines	70	Transair Cambodia	20
Ryukyu Air Commuter	53	Transportes Aéreos de Timor (TAT)	101
Safi	8	Turkmenistan Airlines	105
Saudia	83	Turkuaz	104
Shaheen Air	78	Uni Air	95
Shanghai Airlines Cargo	27	UP	49
Singapore Airlines	85	Uzbekistan Airways	108
Sri Lankan Airlines	89	Vietnam Airlines	109
Sriwijaya Air	40	Viva Macau	64
Sun d'Or	50	Xiamen Airlines	27
Syrian Air	91	Yemenia	112
Taiwan Airlines	95	Yeti Airlines	71

Lost Airline Colours of Asia

AFGHANISTAN
Main gateway: Hamid Karzai International – Kabul

MALCOLM NASON

Ariana Afghan Airlines, 1955–present

Ariana Afghan Airlines (Ariana) is the largest airline in Afghanistan and is also the flag carrier. Founded in 1955, Ariana is the oldest airline in Afghanistan, flying from its main base at Kabul International Airport to India, Russia, Saudi Arabia, Turkey, Kuwait and United Arab Emirates.

It started services, as so many did at that time, with surplus DC3s and also with American support in the shape of Pan Am. As routes expanded in the early 1960s, so did the number and types of aircraft operated. The DC-6A/B and a Convair 340/440 were joined at the end of the decade by the Boeing 727-100. By the end of the 1970s, Ariana's aircraft could be seen as far west as London as well as other European points and had entered the wide-body age with the acquisition of a DC10 (although this was later sold

THOMAS INGENDORN

Lost Airline Colours of Asia

in favour of two Tupolev TU154s). They also provided a considerable amount of seats for the annual Hadj pilgrimage. All of this bringing a peak in the airline's operations.

September 11, 2001, of course, changed everything for the airline. In the conflict that followed, only two aircraft remained intact at the end, and traffic had fallen away to near zero. The airline is currently rebuilding with both Boeing and Airbus products.

The colour scheme has always had a blue theme to it, representing lapis lazuli found in the mountains of the country. The logo has been the same ever since it was first introduced, having been designed by the then Shah of Afghanistan; it represents an Afghan swallow.

Safi, 2006–2016

Safi was the first privately-owned airline in Afghanistan. Having been founded in 2006, it took until 2009 before the first service, utilising a 737-300, took off from Kabul to Frankfurt. An A340-300 quickly followed.

However, it was nearly as quickly phased out following the initiation of a European Union (EU) ban on all Afghan carriers flying into Europe in 2010. It was consequently lifted for Safi, however, in 2012.

Regional routes were still in operation though, and in 2011 the 737s were replaced with the Airbus A320 and later the A319. The airline has also operated the Boeing 767-200. The end came in 2016 when it was grounded over unpaid debts.

THOMAS INGENDORN

ARMENIA
Main gateway: Zvarnots International – Yerevan

Armenian Airlines, 1991–2003

This airline was formed from the bones of Aeroflot's Armenian directorate following the country's independence in 1991. As was the case with many operators in the area, the initial fleet consisted of Soviet types such as Antonov AN12, Tupolev TU135/154 and Ilyushin IL86. However, just seven years later after a period of profitability, financial woes began to emerge. Russia was in the grip of a financial crisis. The airline had technical problems, with its sole A310 acquired to enable flights to the EU after its Soviet types had been banned from European skies. A link-up with Belgian outfit VG Airlines helped for a time, but with the bankruptcy of this carrier in 2002, this just added to Armenian's difficulties. It is also thought that the awarding of many of Armenian Airlines' routes to competitor Armavia was the final blow and the operator went bankrupt in 2003.

THOMAS INGENDORN

Lost Airline Colours of Asia

THOMAS INGENDORN

Amavia, 2001–2013

Starting operations in 2001, with a single Tupolev TU134, it initially operated alongside the then flag carrier, Armenian Airlines. In 2002, the money behind the S7 group bought into the airline, and very quickly the carrier received its first A320 via Siberian Airlines and many of the routes of Armenian Airlines. A year later and the fleet had increased to three and been joined by an ATR42. However, this was soon returned to the lessor, as it did not meet the needs of the airline.

In late 2004, the airline unveiled a new Landor-designed livery incorporating the country's emblem and national colours.

2006 was a bad year for the airline with the crash of one of its A320s with the loss of all on board and a hangar fire which destroyed another A320, leading to what appeared to be a loss of confidence in the airline as passenger numbers fell considerably.

The following years saw the passenger figures bounce back, and in 2011 it became the first airline to operate the Sukhoi Superjet 100, although this honour turned sour the following year with the airline cancelling the second example it had on order and returning the initial aircraft to Sukhoi citing safety concerns, only agreeing to take it back two months later. (It also operated the Canadair CRJ200.)

The financial pressures that had been slowly increasing for the airline and its backers from this time came to a head in 2013 when the airline filed for bankruptcy, subsequently ceasing operations.

AZERBAIJAN
Main gateway: Heydar Aliyev International – Baku

MALCOLM NASON

Azerbaijan Airlines, 1992–present

Another airline formed from the remnants of an Aeroflot division, Azerbaijan Airlines was officially established in 1992. Inheriting a large and diverse fleet of Soviet types, the airline was quick to look west and leased a pair of Boeing 727s to complement the rather less efficient Tupolevs. Routes were mainly regional but reached Europe, including London. In 2000, the 757 was introduced, bringing a new level of comfort, range and payload to the still-young carrier, enabling long-haul routes to be operated more efficiently as well as promoting a more modern image to the rest of the world. Fleet renewal continued with its first Airbus, the A320, in 2010, the 767 arriving in 2011, the A340 in 2013 and the 787-8 in 2014. Its latest addition being a 777-200 to be added to its considerable VIP fleet.

It has operated quite a range of different aircraft over the years including the Antonov AN140 and has the Irkut MC-21-300 on order to complement a fleet that has settled on those mentioned above. The striking blue livery seen on the fleet today was first seen in 2013.

THOMAS INGENDORN

Lost Airline Colours of Asia

BAHRAIN
Main gateway: Bahrain International – Muharraq

Gulf Air, 1950–present

Gulf Air's origins can actually be traced back to the late 1940s when the airline's founder was operating an air taxi service. Gulf Aviation, as it was then, started out with the Avro Anson and de Havilland DH.86B. Soon after, the British Overseas Airways Corporation (BOAC) purchased a large shareholding in the airline, and with it came the British airline's expertise and an increase

in the network and fleet. Twenty years later, this shareholding, along with the remainder, was purchased by the governments of Bahrain, Qatar, Abu Dhabi and Oman to become the flag carrier for all four states under the Gulf Air brand. Within five years, the airline had

Lost Airline Colours of Asia

become an all-jet operation with a mixed fleet comprising the Lockheed L1011 Tristar, Boeing 737-200, Vickers VC10 and BAC 1-11s, although the latter two were already looking at retirement.

The late 1990s and early 2000s was a significant time for the airline with the arrival of the Boeing 767 and Airbus A330/340. Qatar became the first of the four nations to withdraw from the treaty when it focussed on Qatar Airways. A new livery was also introduced, replacing the multicoloured stripe with a predominantly gold livery and redesigned golden falcon logo. Later in the decade, the divorce was finalised when Abu Dhabi pulled out to establish Etihad in

Lost Airline Colours of Asia

2006 with Oman also leaving a year later. This meant that Bahrain now took sole control of the airline. This was not a happy divorce, however, with the airline badly in need of restructuring, losing a reported $1m per day.

Restructure they did, and it now operates a mainly Airbus fleet with the only wide body being the 787-9. Since 2018, the airline has started to repaint its aircraft in a new mainly white livery with a larger typeface and a further redesigned logo.

BANGLADESH
Main gateway: Shahjalal International – Dhaka

Biman Bangladesh Airlines, 1972–present

Biman, as the airline is more commonly known, is the flag carrier of Bangladesh with its first international destination being London. It has had its fair share of difficulties over the years including spats with the Federal Aviation Administration over its use of the DC10

and concerns over the Bangladeshi Civil Aviation Authority (CAA) not meeting International Civil Aviation Organization standards leading to additional restrictions being placed on the airline's services to the US. The DC10 has regularly been a topic of interest with Biman, as they were also the last users of the aircraft on passenger services,

Lost Airline Colours of Asia

even operating a series of enthusiast flights.

In addition to the DC10, Biman have used a broad selection of aircraft over the years, from the BAe ATP to the Airbus A310. Currently, the airline operates a near all-Boeing fleet of 737-800s, 777-300ERs and 787-8/9s. Domestic services will be operated by Dash 8 Q400s.

The logo has remained fairly consistent since the airline's inception and is a stylised white stork inside a red circle. Initially, the livery was a dark blue cheatline which extended onto the tail. In 1980, the cheatline colours were changed to red and green to reflect the Bangladeshi flag. It wasn't until 2010 that there was any change, and following a rebranding exercise the livery was changed to mainly green on a white fuselage. There was a change of government at the time, and with new leadership of the country came a halt to this rebrand after just two months. A return was made to the previous red and white cheatline but in a more sweeping, contemporary fashion.

BHUTAN
Main gateway: Paro International – Paro

THOMAS INGENDORN

Drukair, 1983–present

With the country beginning to welcome visitors in 1981, there were also thoughts of having a national airline to bring these visitors in. Operations began just two years later with a Dornier 228-200. The airline's initial route was from the small strip at Paro to Kolkata in India. The approach and weather at Paro can be challenging, and soon the Dornier was seen to be not really up to the task, and a BAe 146-100 replaced it in 1988. This type proved far more reliable for Drukair operations and enabled further services which were concentrated on South and Southeast Asia, including Singapore and Bangkok, with a second example being added in 1992. The airline was to be the launch customer for the Avro RJX-85, but the cancellation of this programme led to the airline looking elsewhere. After looking at a number of options, the Airbus A319 was selected, and, interestingly, it became the largest ever purchase made by the country. Arriving in 2004, in an updated livery, it was joined by a second before the end of the year. In 2011, the ATR42 was introduced to the fleet and, most recently, an Airbus A320neo.

Lost Airline Colours of Asia

BRUNEI
Main gateway: Brunei International – Bandar Seri Begawan

Royal Brunei Airlines, 1975–present

The state-owned national flag carrier of Brunei started operations with a service to Singapore using a Boeing 737-200. Following its independence from the UK in 1984, the airline continued to expand in the region, acquiring the Boeing 757-200 which extended the route structure to the UK. The airline moved into wide-body operations with the arrival of the Boeing 767 and service to Frankfurt. The 767 delivery flight broke a world record, flying non-stop for 17 hours and 22 minutes from Seattle to Nairobi en route to Brunei. For shorter distances, Fokker 50s and 100s were acquired as was the Dornier 228. The new millennium brought with it a re-equipping programme starting with new A319/320s with the 767 being replaced by the 777-200ER, as well as the business being restructured with many routes being axed. With the arrival of the Boeing 787s in 2013 came a new livery consisting of a lighter yellow tail with an all-white fuselage.

CAMBODIA
Main gateway: Phnom Penh International – Phnom Penh

JEAN-LUC ALTHERR

Kampuchea Airlines, 1997–2004

Starting services in 1997 with a Lockheed L1011 and a BAe 146, this airline was operating regional passenger services from its Phnom Penh base. It was briefly known as SK Air and had Orient Thai as a 49% shareholder. It introduced a Boeing 757-200, previously operated by myTravel, just before its collapse in 2004.

Transair Cambodia, 1992–1993

This airline was intended to run regional routes from its proposed Phnom Penh base with a start-up of two HS748s and a single BAe 146-200. However, the aircraft never even made it to the country never mind starting operations with the airline. The allocated aircraft were eventually delivered to other airlines.

CHINA
Main gateway: Beijing Capital International – Beijing

CAAC, 1949–1988

CAAC stands for the Civil Aviation Administration of China and operated a government monopoly in China for nearly 40 years. Starting with just domestic routes, it managed its operations in a similar way to that in which Aeroflot did in the Soviet Union and indeed acquired its aircraft from there until it started to look west following a cooling in Sino–Soviet relations in the early 1960s. The UK was the initial recipient of business when, in 1963, an order was placed for the Vickers Viscount, followed by Hawker Siddeleys Trident eight years later. The carrier even placed a provisional order for three Concordes. Soon after, the airline's eyes moved further west following Nixon's presidential visit in 1972 with Boeing, the recipient of an order for ten 707s, even though the IL62 was still in operation on long-range routes. The route structure until the 1980s was mainly to the Communist Bloc, but in the middle of that decade it spread its wings to most other parts of the globe.

1988 saw a massive change in

Lost Airline Colours of Asia

the way aviation was run in the country. CAAC had from it's early days been split into regional bureaux, and when the airline itself was divided into separate entities, it was based around these regions with one carrier for each of them:

Air China for Beijing, China Eastern for Shanghai, China Northern for Shenyang, China Northwest for Xi'an, China Southern for Guangzhou and China Southwest for Chengdu, all of which are detailed below. In addition, and just prior to the official breakup, trials had been undertaken whereby Xiamen Airlines was formed to operate from the Xiamen special economic zone as well as joint ventures with regional governments in Xinjiang (China Xinjiang Airlines) and Shanghai (Shanghai Airlines). The latter was also in cooperation with local business.

Most of the new airlines operated in some level of hybrid liveries until each could get their own aircraft painted in their own full livery. CAAC continued to operate as a government agency overseeing aviation in the country.

Air China (Beijing), 1988–present

Mentioned simply for completeness as Air China has not changed its livery since its 1988 inception.

China Eastern Airlines (Shanghai), 1988–present

Based in Shanghai, China Eastern is the country's second largest carrier by passenger

numbers after China Southern. It founded China Cargo Airlines in a joint venture with China Ocean Shipping Company, but also over the decades the airline has merged with a number of others including Great Wall Airlines, China Yunnan, China Northwest, China United and latterly Shanghai Airlines although

this airline retained its brand and livery.

China Eastern's livery has changed little over the years with only the initial red and blue cheatline disappearing in 2014 along with a slight change to the logo. There have been quite a number of special liveries worn with topics ranging from Toy Story to Expo 2010. The airline has operated an astonishing number of aircraft over its lifetime. Every Airbus type apart from the A318, every Boeing apart from the 757, with supporting roles from McDonnell Douglas, BAe, Embraer, Fokker and even Yakovlev and Xian, with Comac still to come, as the airline is scheduled to be the launch customer for the C919.

China Northern Airlines (Shenyang), 1988–2003 (China Southern)

Mainly a domestic carrier, its Airbus A300, McDonnell Douglas MD80/90 and latterly the Airbus A321 could also be seen in North and South Korea and Japan. It was also the sole operator of the ill-fated MD90-30T (Trunkliner) – the programme to manufacture the MD90 in China that was initially aimed at producing 40 aircraft but in fact only ever produced two. The carrier only took them

as they already operated the Long Beach constructed version. The initial allocated customer, Shenzen Airlines, having already started operating the Boeing 737-300/-700 was not then prepared to take them when they were eventually ready for delivery.

China Northwest Airlines (Xi'an), 1988–2002 (China Eastern)

The last of the original six to take up its own identity of blue and red cheatlines and a logo comprising a globe and a Feitan goddess. This livery was eventually seen on a variety of aircraft including Airbus A310, A300 and A320 (this latter type replacing the older Tupolev TU154) as well as on its regional division's BAe 146-100 and Y-7s.

It's routes were mainly domestic but with some international ones, again mainly to Japan. The airline has the dubious honour of having the deadliest aviation accident to occur in mainland China as part of its history. It was absorbed into China Eastern following the rationalisation of the Chinese aviation scene in 2002, subsequently operating as China Eastern Xi Bei.

China Southern Airlines (Guangzhou),1988–present

Mentioned simply for completeness as China Southern has not changed its livery since its 1988 inception.

China Southwest Airlines (Chengdu), 1988–2002 (Air China)

Based in Chengdu, the airline operated a mainly Boeing fleet of 707s, 737s and 757s but had also operated IL18s and TU154s in it's early days as well as, in its later years, three A340-300s originally destined for China Eastern. The airline flew domestic sectors mainly, for which it added the Y-7 but also had some regional routes within Asia. In the 2002 Chinese aviation industry consolidation, China Southwest was absorbed into Air China.

China Express Airlines, 2006–present

Based at Chongqing, China Express is China's first private regional airline. It survived a scare just a few years into its existence when, after a couple of incidents, the Chinese authorities ordered the airline to suspend operations for a period of time. Initially operating the Canadair CRJ 200, these

were completely replaced by the larger CRJ900 by 2015. The aircraft size continues to grow, with the airline acquiring the A320, and the A320neo just about to be delivered in a modified livery which sees larger titles and tail logo and the removal of the logo from the forward fuselage.

Great Wall Airlines, 2006–2011 (China Cargo Airlines)

Co-owned by, amongst others, China Eastern this Shanghai-based all-cargo outfit started operations in 2006 with a service to Amsterdam. After just two months though, all operations were suspended when the parent company, China Great Wall Industry, had sanctions imposed by the USA due to alleged transfer of missile technology to Iran. With no ability to operate, the airline returned its aircraft to SIA Cargo until operations resumed in December, following the lifting of the sanctions. Destinations were resumed to Amsterdam, Mumbai/Chennai and Incheon. New destinations to Manchester, Chicago, Atlanta and Seattle started being introduced in 2007. In 2011, the airline was merged into China Cargo Airlines created by China Eastern, Great Wall's majority shareholder.

Shanghai Airlines Cargo, 2006–2010 (China Cargo Airlines)

With the assistance of EVA Air of Taiwan, Shanghai Airlines Cargo entered the local cargo market in 2006 operating a fleet of Boeing 737-300Fs, 757-200Fs and McDonnell Douglas MD11Fs in a livery similar to the passenger airline. Although starting with routes in the region, the airline expanded out to the USA and Europe before the merging of China Eastern and Shanghai Airlines started a consolidation with the former's cargo arms, Great Wall Airlines and China Cargo under the latter banner.

Xiamen Airlines, 1984–present

Formed just prior to the breakup of CAAC, it is now owned in part by China Southern Airlines. Initially just a domestic carrier linking its home province of Fujian with the rest of the country, it has always been a solely Boeing operator starting out with the 737-200. It went on to operate the -300/-500/-700/-800 and MAX8 variants as well as the 757-200 and 787-8/-9. This latter aircraft enabling the carrier to operate long-haul routes, starting with Amsterdam in Europe, quickly followed by Sydney and then onto the North American continent to Vancouver followed by Seattle, Los Angeles and New York. Its two previous liveries were very similar, consisting of a multiple blue cheatline and bird logo in a blue circle, until the more recent all-blue tail livery. It became a Star Alliance member in 2012.

GEORGIA
Main gateway: Tbilisi International – Tbilisi

THOMAS INGENDORN

Fly Georgia, 2012–2013
This privately-owned airline became the second national airline of Georgia when it started operations in 2012 with a service from Tbilisi to Amsterdam utilising an Airbus A319. It ordered two of the larger A320 with intentions to start services to destinations in Europe and the Middle East. However, after just 14 months in the air, the Georgian authorities suspended the airline's licence, effectively grounding the fledgling carrier.

FlyVista, 2014–2015
Another short-lived Georgian operator, FlyVista possibly suffered from a case of bad timing. This thought is due to one of its important routes, that of Kiev in the Ukraine, suffering as a result of the Ukraine crisis. The subsequent fall in passenger numbers on this and its other routes lead to its 737-300s being grounded and all operations ceasing.

MALCOLM NASON

Lost Airline Colours of Asia

HONG KONG
Main gateway: Chek Lap Kok Hong Kong International – Hong Kong

Air Hong Kong, 1988–present

Commencing operations in 1988 with a Boeing 707 freighter on charter services to India and the UK. The arrival of a second 707 two years later enabled scheduled services to start to Manchester which remained an important destination for many years. In 1994, Cathay Pacific acquired a controlling stake in the airline, by which time the 747-100SF had been introduced.

Into the new millennium and the 707s had left the fleet, and operations had been scaled back, dropping Manchester and Brussels with the focus now on Asian destinations. After purchasing the airline outright, Cathay then entered into a joint venture with DHL selling 30% to them, which released funds to purchase new aircraft. In fact, the airline became the launch customer for the A300-600F freighter. This joint

venture also created a different look from the previous two. The livery worn by the current fleet of A300s and A330s (but also worn by the previously operated 747-400BCF) now advertises this venture and comprises a mainly white front fuselage section, a change of titles, the removal of the Air Hong Kong logo and the addition of a yellow rear and tail section and smaller DHL titles. This, despite Cathay regaining full control of the airline.

Cathay Pacific, 1946–present

This airline was founded by two pilots, who had flown with the China National Aviation Corporation during the Second World War, using a single DC3 named 'Betty' and with the idea to fly essential goods from Australia to China following the end of the war. Cathay Pacific was originally based in Shanghai but due to operating difficulties there, moved to Hong Kong after just a few months. It was soon after this that one of its current major shareholders, Swire Pacific, then known as John Swire and Sons, first became involved.

The airline prospered over the coming decades, purchasing Hong Kong Airways in 1959 and so becoming the dominant airline in the then British colony.

The 'Lettuce green', or as it was officially known 'Brunswick green', livery was first seen with the arrival of the airline's first 707 in 1971 and went on to be worn on further jets, such as the Convair 880, Lockheed Tristar and Boeing 747, as the fleet and route structure grew.

With the handover of Hong Kong back to China in 1994, registrations changed from the

'VR' prefix to the Chinese standard 'B'.

The 1990s also saw the acquisition of significant stakes in Dragonair and Air Hong Kong which eventually saw these two airlines' identities change somewhat. As well as this, the airline embarked on a fleet replacement programme and with it the 'Brushwing' new livery and logo seen on the new Boeing 777s and later on Airbus A330s/340s. In 2014, this livery was updated to the current design which, although similar, now has an all-green tail but still with the brushwing logo. The airline has been no stranger to special liveries, often promoting Hong Kong as a destination for business and leisure. Its freighters have also occasionally been seen in non-standard schemes.

Dragonair, 1985–2016 (Cathay Dragon)

Starting with a single 737 and a service to Malaysia, Dragonair was the first Hong Kong-based airline to compete with Cathay Pacific – something that was to hinder early expansion plans as the Hong Kong government adopted a 'one route, one airline' policy, meaning it was not able to gain the route licences it wished, and felt it needed, to compete.

In the 1990s, this issue became less of a problem as their erstwhile competitor became part owner, and some of Cathay's routes were transferred to Dragonair as part of a period of cooperation between British-backed Cathay and mainland China. An L1011 was transferred to Dragonair to operate to mainland China, as this was to be the focus of expansion for the newly acquired subsidiary.

In the early 1990s, a move towards an all-Airbus fleet began with the arrival of A320s and later, A330s.

Cargo was also a major part of the company's business and in 2000 it leased 747s on routes to China, Europe and the Middle East with these and the passenger services showing excellent growth and again putting them in competition with its bigger shareholder. In 2006 Dragonair became a wholly owned subsidiary of Cathay and expansion plans had been reined in with the airline eventually being rebranded as Cathay Dragon in 2016. Following the initial red tail and cheatline the airline had a mainly white livery, only changing at the above mentioned rebranding.

SPENCER BENNETT

Hong Kong Express, 2004–present

Founded by a Macau-based casino owner, Hong Kong Express became the fourth passenger airline based in the territory. It initially operated the Embraer E170 on services into mainland China, adding the 737-800 approximately 18 months later. In 2006, the HNA Group purchased a significant stake in the airline leading to expansion in routes and a change of livery from the initial, somewhat basic white version to one similar to all HNA Group airlines. In 2013, the airline announced that it was to transform into a low-cost carrier (LCC), change its name to HK Express and introduce and rationalise on a new aircraft type, the Airbus A320. This new direction also brought with it a new colourful livery based on the Hong Kong city skyline. In 2019, Cathay Pacific completed the purchase of the airline but stated that it will remain as a standalone LCC airline.

SPENCER BENNETT

INDIA
Main gateway: Chhatrapati Rajaram Maharaj Airport – Mumbai

Air India, 1979–present

Approaching its 90th birthday, Air India has seen a lot of change. Formed in 1932 as Tata Airlines, it now operates a large mixed Airbus/Boeing fleet on its domestic and international route structure, alongside its subsidiaries Air India Regional and Air India Express. It was the first Asian airline to enter the jet age when it received its first 707 in 1960, going on to become the world's first all-jet airline in 1962. The original logo was of a centaur, designed to represent Sagittarius shooting an arrow through the Wheel of Konark; this logo remained until the current livery was introduced. The first 'Palace in the Sky' livery being introduced in 1971 with the arrival of the 747. The basis of its livery has always been mainly red and white, generally with a red palace-style design around each window. However, in 1989 the airline introduced a supplement to this livery which consisted of a gold disc-like design on a broad red stripe but doing away with the palace markings. A 747 was the first aircraft to be painted in this livery. In 2007 though, the 'Palace in the Sky' was reintroduced along with a new (and its current) logo.

Lost Airline Colours of Asia

Jet Airways, 1993–2019

At one time the largest commercial passenger airline in India, Jet Airways suffered from a considerable amount of low-cost competition, eventually losing this accolade to IndiGo in 2017. It was the first airline in Southeast Asia to order the 737-800 when it announced an order for ten at the 1999 Paris Air Show. Long-haul operations started in May 2005 with an A340-300 leased from South African Airways. Expansion into other routes brought with it further aircraft in the form of the Airbus A330 and Boeing 777. In 2007, Air Sahara was taken over and rebranded as JetLite, although just over a year later it was integrated into the main fleet. The airline tried again in 2009, this time naming the carrier Jet Konnect. Both of these carriers sported the same livery except for titles. It utilised the same logo as the parent but with a light blue colour covering both the tail and half the fuselage.

The main airline livery has changed little over its lifetime with the initial straight cheatline morphing in 2007 into a more flowing, ribbon-like version and the title font changing and getting larger. The airline finally folded in 2019, but there is hope in some areas that it can be resurrected in some form.

Kingfisher Airlines, 2005–2012

Starting out with four Airbus A320s on domestic routes, Kingfisher never made a profit in its entire, and somewhat troubled, existence, despite at one time achieving the second largest share of India's domestic market. In an attempt to start international services early (Indian airlines cannot operate abroad until they have been in business for five years), it bought out Air Deccan in 2007. However, it was this purchase that is thought to have been the final straw. Name changes and a short-lived foray into LCC operations did nothing to stem losses, and by 2012 things had culminated in staff on strike, aircraft grounded and an unmanageable debt leading to frozen bank accounts and the suspension of its licence, with the airlines owner seemingly fleeing the country to avoid prosecution. The airline had operated the ATR42/72 in addition to the A320 family on regional and domestic routes with the A330 on the London route. Five A340s had been ordered but never delivered.

INDONESIA
Main gateway: Hakim Perdanakusuma International Airport – Jakarta

Garuda Indonesia, 1949–present

After some commercial flights run by the Indonesian Air Force and following discussions with KLM over the use of staff from their Dutch East Indies subsidiary, the newly named Garuda Indonesian Airways was formed. Soon after, in December 1949, two DC3s arrived and these legendary aircraft formed the backbone of the new airline, eventually with 22 in the fleet. It took until 1965 for the airline to stretch its wings as far as Europe, and it was no surprise that Amsterdam was the first destination on the continent. This new market and others was facilitated by Garuda's entry into the jet age with the arrival of the DC8. Over 40 years later this new market was denied to Garuda after the EU banned all airlines from Indonesia from flying in. The ban was lifted in 2009. The word 'Garuda' is Sanskrit for a mythical bird-like creature from the Hindi, Buddhist and Jain faiths. Therefore, it is no surprise that a stylised version forms a significant part of the airline's current livery. However, it was not always the

case. Originally, aircraft simply had a cheatline of blue lines with Indonesia Airways titles. In the 1960s, the airline moved to red for its colour scheme and the first addition of a bird-like logo on the tail (this livery is currently worn by a 737-800). The 1970s brought another change – the red cheatline remains but is extended up the tail with the logo replaced with the word 'Garuda' (this livery has also been brought back and is currently on a 777-300). 1985 brought a further, and much greater, change. The red was replaced with blues; the name was changed to Garuda Indonesia, and the logo became much more prominent and more bird-like, again. In 2009, yet another rebranding exercise was undertaken, bringing in the livery we see today. The colour palette remains blue and aqua, but it is now mainly on the tail, replacing the logo in what is described as 'nature's wing'.

Merpati Nusantara Airlines, 1962–2014

Set up as a second state airline with the intention of serving domestic routes previously operated by the Air Force, who also provided two DC3s as part of the start-up fleet. In 1978, the airline was taken over by Garuda but continued to operate under its own banner. In 1992, the airline took delivery of the BAe ATP to operate domestic routes. The airline has operated an extensive list as diverse as the Boeing 707, Xian MA60 and Lockheed L100. Its employees were, in part, the catalyst for the airline's demise when in 2014, after having not been paid for three months,

many of them resigned making it difficult to operate. However, by then its cashflow problems had already hampered its ability to operate, with the airline having already been denied fuel on credit, and in February 2014 all services were suspended. There have been hopes for a relaunch with the last being back in 2018 utilising 737-800, but the impact on the world's airlines from the Covid-19 virus will surely be the final chapter in this story.

Sriwijaya Air 2003 - present

PT Sriwijaya Air is a private company and the third largest airline in the country. Initial aircraft was the Boeing 737-200. It is this type that has remained the fleet choice ever since with the airline operating the -300 and -400 in the past with the current fleet comprising the -500, -800 and -900ER.

Its first flights were from Jakarta to Pangkal Pinang, Jakarta to Palembang, Jakarta to Jambi, and Jakarta to Pontianak. Currently, Sriwijaya Air Group has 47 aircraft operating on a total of 53 routes.

AEROPRINTS.COM CC BY-SA 3.0

In service terms the airline sits just above the low-cost trend as it serves light snacks. However, there are plans to move into becoming a full-service airline. Its initial livery consisted of a red and blue cheatline with the blue extending up on the tail which had the logo. Later this was updated moving the blue and red to just the rear of the aircraft with a more stylised version of the tail logo. In 2020 the airline made a further change. It replaced the Sriwijaya Air titles with a large 'SJ' with the addition of its web address. Every Sriwijaya Air Group aircraft (including its subsidiary NAM Air) has a unique name based on holy book phrases, places, behaviours and even plants or birds.

SPENCER BENNETT

Tigerair Mandala, 2012–2014

This airline's roots go way back to 1969, when an operation linked with the Indonesian Army was created to operate domestic services around the country. It wasn't until 1992 that it retired the last of its turboprop fleet of Vickers Viscounts and Lockheed Electras, replacing them with second-hand Boeings. It suffered a major financial scandal when one military officer managed to extract $13.5m out of the company funds. At the same time, the political situation in the country led to the military having to remove its control of businesses in the country, whilst at the same time the Indonesian government was unwilling or unable to take control. Subsequently, a consortium which had IndiGo as a partner took control and within a year had changed this rather staid company into a modern airline and most importantly a safe one enabling it to operate as a Category 1 airline with regards to safety unlike others in the country, including the flag carrier.

A320s were introduced in 2009, but under two years later all services were suspended due to mounting debts. It wasn't until April 2012 that, after the formation of a new group including Singapore-based Tiger Airways, the airline, now as an LCC, took to the skies, this time with the Tiger Airways branding and a name change. This meant that the previous design of a gold and blue eight-pointed lotus-like logo was replaced with the familiar Tigerair striped tail but with Mandala titles.

IRAN
Main gateway: Imam Khomeini International Airport – Tehran

JEAN-LUC ALTHERR

Iran Air, 1944–present

Starting towards the end of the Second World War as Iranian Airlines and operating DC3s as far as Baghdad and Beirut, the airline expanded into the 1950s with DC4s, Convair 240s and Vickers Viscounts on routes to the west of the region. In 1961, the Iranian government decreed that a state airline should be created, and to facilitate this, Iranian Airways was merged with Persian Air Services to form United Iranian Airlines. Later it was renamed Iranian National Airlines Corporation but very soon just became known as Iran Air. This time also saw the creation of the airline's emblem: the Homa bird, a mythical creature said to be the bearer of good fortune. In a somewhat now-ironic twist, the US government, seeking to reduce Soviet influences in the region provided $1.5m for the airline's

Lost Airline Colours of Asia

redevelopment, a figure over $8.5m at today's value. The airline was careful in its expansion, starting by adding jets in 1965 with Boeings 707 and 727, moving on to the 737 in 1971 and the 747 including the SP (special performance) version in 1978. Such was its financial prudence that it had made a profit every year since 1962 allowing for the purchase of these modern aircraft and indeed placed an order for a Concorde, which was later cancelled of course!

The late 1970s and early 1980s saw the start of a troubled and difficult time for the airline with the Iran–Iraq War and the occupation of the US embassy in Tehran leading to US sanctions which would last for two decades. Despite this, the airline still managed to keep going, receiving two A300B4s, but these and the rest of the fleet were slowly becoming less reliable due to lack of spares. In 2010, by which time A320s had been acquired, the EU banned all Iran Air flights due to safety concerns. There was a brief period of respite when the Obama administration lifted sanctions leading to a large order, spread across Airbus, Boeing and ATR, but only the ATR aircraft were ever delivered as President Trump reinstated the sanctions in 2018. The airline's livery has always been a mix of blue and white in differing amounts, using the Homa bird as the tail logo.

Iran Aseman Airlines, 1980–present

Another airline to suffer from US sanctions is Iran Aseman, being also unable to fly into the EU or USA. Much younger than its government-owned rival, this airline operated a number of different types over its 40 years in the air including various Fokker and ATR types, with the ATR72 still in use. It also still operates the 737-400 and previously the 727 for which it had the honour of operating the final ever commercial passenger service in the world on January 13, 2019. The current fleet, in addition to that already mentioned, consists of the Fokker 100 and Airbus A320/340. The airline's livery is, and has always consisted of, different shades of blue stripes which used to run up the tail but now form a flowing ribbon along the side of the aircraft. The logo, which also resembles a bird, now sits on an all-white tail.

Kish Airlines, 1990–present

Operating scheduled and charter services, both internationally and domestically, from Kish Island and owned by various Kish Island organisations, this niche operator started operations with TU154s and MD80/83s, and later Yak 42Ds. The carrier became the first private company in Iran to receive its air operating certificate (AOC) from the Iranian civil aviation agency. The airline soon ran into financial difficulties leading to a change of management. Having survived this time, the airline now operates the Fokker 100, McDonnell Douglas MD82/83 and the Airbus A321 in a modified livery which now includes red stripes near to and extending onto the tail.

IRAQ
Main gateway: Baghdad International Airport – Baghdad

MALCOLM NASON

Iraqi Airways, 1945–present

Another Middle Eastern airline to be created at the end of the Second World War, Iraqi Airways started operations with the de Havilland Dragon Rapide, moving on to Vickers Viscounts which performed the majority of services until the arrival of the 1960s jet age in the form of the Tupolev TU124 and Hawker Siddeley Tridents, and latterly the Ilyushin IL76 hauling cargo, all of which stretched the route map across the Middle East, Africa and Europe. These early aircraft, with the exception of the IL76, had a very simple livery of a green cheatline with the Iraqi flag on the tail, before moving on to the dramatic two-tone green livery which was in place until the current livery replaced it in 2012. (A new blue livery intended to become the standard was revealed in 2008 but was axed after just a single CRJ had been painted.) With the granting of a route licence to John F. Kennedy International Airport in 1970, the

JEAN-LUC ALTHERR

Lost Airline Colours of Asia

JEAN-LUC ALTHERR

airline turned to Boeing and the 707 for an aircraft able to fly the route, with the 747 arriving later in the decade. Largley unaffected by the Iran–Iraq War throughout most of the 1980s, the airline kept flying, adding both new aircraft types (727 and A310) and routes until 1991 when, having ferried all its aircraft away from the country to secret destinations, Iraq invaded Kuwait. Following the failure of this venture, the airline was grounded, to all but domestic operations, by UN sanctions. However, even domestic services were patchy to say the least, as the US and UK had imposed a no-fly zone over the country. It would take until 2004 for the airline to resume international services with a flight to Amman in Jordan. Following the re-introduction of services, new aircraft were acquired including various models of the 737 and in more recent years CRJ900 and 767/777, with the most recent being the A320/321/330, with A220 and 787 on order. Service into Europe has been fraught with difficulties, with services starting but then being cancelled due to the airline not meeting safety standards, a situation going back and forth throughout the decade.

THOMAS INGENDORN

JEAN-LUC ALTHERR

Lost Airline Colours of Asia

ISRAEL
Main gateway: Ben Gurion Airport – Tel Aviv

Arkia, 1949–present

When the then new state of Israel was created in 1948, it soon became clear that there was a demand for an airline linking the capital with the regions. Founded in 1949, Israel Inland Airlines, as it was originally known, commenced operations in 1950 with DH.89s followed by Curtis Commanders and DC3s. The port city of Eilat in the south of the country was a major destination for the airline from its Tel Aviv base, and as the city grew so did the airline. In the 1980s, it merged with Kanaf Airlines and expanded into the international charter market. Following the Israeli government awarding it its scheduled operator's licence in 2007 for services to Dublin and Larnaca, the airline announced its intentions to open up more scheduled routes including long haul to New York and Bangkok. The fleet of 737s, 757s and ATR 72s were simply not fit for this new role, and the airline moved initially to the Embraer 190/195 then adding the A321LR, for whom it later became the launch customer. It currently has the A330-800neo on order. Previous liveries have, in the main, reflected the light blue of the country's flag with additional orange trim. However, with the arrival of the A321LR, a new much bolder livery and logo has appeared and in differing colours.

Lost Airline Colours of Asia

El Al, 1949–present

Founded at the same time as the new country it represents and named from a passage in the Hebrew Bible, El Al started operational service (a symbolic maiden flight bringing the first Israeli President home from Geneva occurred a year earlier) with a flight to Rome and Paris. The airline continued to grow alongside the country, utilising a variety of prop types including the Lockheed Constellation with which it became the first airline outside Europe and the US to operate a scheduled trans-Atlantic service (albeit with multiple stops), the Curtis Commando

(for cargo) and their first type, the DC4, which was seen increasingly at European destinations.

Early liveries comprised a combination of the Israeli flag on the tail and a cheatline with a winged logo. It wasn't until 1961 and the arrival of the jet age that the more consistent and longer lasting two-tone blue livery was adopted, this livery remaining current for nearly three decades. This time also saw the airline become profitable, with over half of passengers arriving in the country doing so on an El Al flight.

More Boeings arrived over the coming decades with the 747 in 1971, 737 in 1980, 767 in 1983 and 757 in 1987. The airline going on to replace these with newer 737-800s and 777s, and 787s for longer-haul services, in more recent times.

Political tensions have always led to the airline being ultra cautious in its security measures, with all aircraft being fitted with anti-missile technologies since 2000. The current blue and silver ribbons livery arrived in 1998 coinciding with the airline's 50th anniversary.

MAOF, 1981–1984

It could be said that the roots of MAOF actually go back to 1969 when an air taxi operation of the same name had been created by the founder of the airline proper. MAOF was the first independent charter airline in Israel. It initially operated Boeing 720s on services throughout Europe, joined later by the 707. El Al were not happy with the competition and embarked on a programme aimed at removing this upstart. In addition, Israel invaded neighbouring Lebanon in 1982 which brought with it further economic difficulties resulting in bankruptcy in late 1984, ending MAOF's short life.

UP, 2014–2018

UP by El Al, as the airline was marketed by its parent company, was first unveiled in 2013 as its low-cost brand. Operations commenced in 2014, with Boeing 737-800s transferred from the mainline fleet. The route structure was quite limited and consisted of services that had all once been operated by El Al, with just five destinations across Europe from Larnaca in the east to Berlin in the west. However, the experiment never really worked and operations ceased in late 2018, with the distinctive clouds and sky livery eventually disappearing in favour of the rather dull mainline white.

Sun d'Or, 1977–present

When the airline was first incorporated as an El Al subsidiary, it was called El Al Charter Services Ltd, and it wasn't until four years later that the name Sun d'Or International Airlines Ltd was adopted. Mainly operating charter holiday flights, the airline started with Boeing 707s until later moving on to the Boeing 757-200. In 2005, El Al was privatised, with Sun D'Or becoming a private company at the same time although remaining a fully owned subsidiary of El Al. Liveries have varied over the years from variants of the parent to a much darker blue. In 2011, the airline's operating licence was revoked on the grounds of non-compliance of management standards, leading to all future flights being operated with El Al aircraft although with the new 'Sunny' cartoon-like chick logo.

JAPAN
Main gateway: Narita International Airport – Tokyo

Amakusa Airlines, 2000–present

Having been first established in 1998, this Japanese regional airline first took to the skies in March 2000 with a single de Havilland Dash 8 in this dolphin-themed livery. It has quite a limited route structure focusing on services from its home at Amakusa to Kunamoto, both on the island of Kyushu. In 2016, the airline moved from the Dash 8 to ATR42-600s, although the livery had already been changed to the current scheme. It is still dolphin themed but now with a single animal covering the whole aircraft in addition to a replica on each engine.

Japan Airlines (JAL), 1951–present

ROY CARTLEDGE

Initially founded in 1951 and operating domestic services with a Martin 202, this private airline had all its assets assumed by the Japanese government to form a new state-owned airline, with international services starting just the following year. The airline operated a number of Douglas prop aircraft and when it came to the jet age, kept with the Long Beach manufacturer when it took delivery of the DC8 in 1960. In the

Lost Airline Colours of Asia

1970s the DC10 arrived, but in addition Boeing gained a foothold supplying the 727 and 747. More Boeings arrived in the form of 737 and 767 through the following decades, as well as the MD11. The new millennium brought with it a merger with Japan Air System and a period of bankruptcy protection.

It wasn't until the arrival of the DC8 that the JAL Tsurumaru crane circle logo was introduced and which remained, albeit with the introduction of new titles in the form of a JAL logo, until 2002 when the 'Arc of the Sun' livery was introduced with it's mainly red tail and yet another JAL logo which remained until 2011 when the Tsurumaru was reintroduced, as was full Japan Airlines titles. Well known for special liveries, the airline has had aircraft featuring Disneyland, sports teams, films and holiday destinations such as its Super Resort Express.

Nippon Cargo Airlines, 1985–present

Created by All Nippon Airways (ANA) and six different ocean shipping companies, it took a number of years of negotiations before the first flight took place. The airline has now expanded its operations into cities in Asia, America and Europe. Nippon Cargo has always been a 747 operator of various marques, with the current fleet comprising just the 8F variant. ANA sold its stake in 2005, and it is now 10% owned by shipping company Nippon Yusen.

The original livery was chosen via a competition, with the winning design having the strap-line "Ocean and sky Now As one" signifying the relationship between the forming partners. The two blues are said to signify the colours of the ocean and the sky. A 'Green Freighter' livery was introduced in 2007 and named NCA Pegasus. With the arrival of the first 747-8F, Nippon Cargo Airlines introduced a new livery which kept the blues of the earlier design but added a single red stripe, all in a more flowing manner than seen previously.

Ryukyu Air Commuter, 1985–present

This small domestic Japanese operator based on the island of Okinawa and owned in part by the local government. The airline has only operated two aircraft types, the BN-2 Islander and the de Havilland Dash 8, of which it has operated three different variants. Currently it has five Q400s painted in a livery comprising Ryukyu Air Commuter titles and a JAL logo on the tail of an otherwise all-white aircraft. Previously, another hybrid livery of titles plus a JAL tail and styling were worn on the Q300s around 2009, but the original livery seen here is the only full Ryukyu colour scheme known to have been worn.

JORDAN
Main gateway: Queen Alia International Airport – Amman

JEAN-LUC ALTHERR

Royal Jordanian, 1963–present

Established in 1963 by the then King Hussain of Jordan and named after his eldest child, Alia, it was originally a private airline although later taken over by the Jordanian government and established as the country's flag carrier. Regional services with DC7s and Handley Page Heralds were the initial operations, later moving into Europe with a service to Rome. Despite the loss of one DC7 from an Israeli air strike during the Six-Day War, the airline continued to expand and in 1968 took delivery of its first jet, the Sud Aviation Caravelle. It's early livery was very much of the time, consisting of a cheatline over the windows, extending up the tail

JEAN-LUC ALTHERR   JEAN-LUC ALTHERR

Lost Airline Colours of Asia

JEAN-LUC ALTHERR

with titles both on the fuselage and tail. In Alia's case, the colours were orange and gold. The 1970s saw the introduction of many of Boeing's offerings, initially the 707 and later 720s, 727s and right up to the 747. In the 1980s, further expansion occurred and also a move away from an all-Boeing fleet with the introduction of the Lockheed L1011 and A310s and A320s from Airbus. Around the same time, a new name,

MALCOLM NASON

Royal Jordanian, was introduced along with a new livery, making both the tail and underside of the aircraft mainly red with a crown logo on the tail also. There was a short-lived grey trial livery applied to one of the Tristars, but it never made it to become the airline's new standard. By the turn of the millennium, the airline had turned its thoughts to fleet renewal and about becoming the first Arab airline to join an alliance when it became part of Oneworld. It had also changed its livery once again to what is seen currently.

KAZAKHSTAN
Main gateway: Almaty International Airport – Almaty

Air Astana, 2002–present

The flag carrier of Kazakhstan commenced operations in 2002 with particularly interesting parentage, as it is jointly owned by BAe Systems at the request of the then Kazahk president. Reporting a profit in its first full year of operations, it was just the following year that it became the flag carrier upon the demise of the previous incumbent, Air Kazakhstan, rapidly expanding from its original, purely domestic, routes to the likes of Dubai, Beijing, Istanbul and later Frankfurt and London, it being the only Kazakh airline allowed into the EU at the time. Despite having a substantial investment, the airline never operated any BAe aircraft and has now moved from the original 737 and F50s to a large mixed Airbus/Boeing/Embraer fleet The livery has remained very similar since inception, with the only major change being the loss of the white part of the logo on the tail, meaning I could incorporate it into the book!

Lost Airline Colours of Asia

KUWAIT
Main gateway: Kuwait International Airport – Kuwait City

Kuwait Airways, 1954–present

As with many an airline starting in the years following the Second World War, operations began with the Douglas DC3 on routes to neighbouring countries. The route network was expanded throughout the region with the addition of the Vickers Viscount, and following the country's independence from Great Britain in 1961 acquired full control of the airline whilst, at the same time, absorbing rival Trans Arabia Airways which it also controlled. De Havilland Comets heralded the arrival of the jet age in 1962, later supplemented by BAC 1-11s, Hawker Siddeley Tridents and Boeings offerings at the time the 707, 727, 737 and, of course, the ubiquitous 747. Into the 1980s and the first Airbus, whose aircraft would eventually form the vast majority of the current fleet, arrived in the shape of the A300/310. The invasion of Kuwait by Iraqi forces in 1990 decimated the airline's fleet with aircraft either destroyed or seized by the Iraqis leaving just nine, which were out of the

country at the time of the invasion, available after hostilities ended. New aircraft in the form of Airbus A330s/340s/320s and the Boeing 777 were ordered and the route network expanded as they arrived. Many of the types remain, with the exception of the A340 and indeed newer Airbus aircraft are currently arriving or are on order including being the launch customer for the A330-800neo. The airline's livery has changed little over the years, being variations on the theme of a blue cheatline and blue banner with the stylised bird logo within, only changing when the current, more contemporary looking, livery was introduced in 2016.

KYRGYZSTAN
Main gateway: Manas International Airport – Bishkek

Air Kyrgyzstan, 2001–present
Originally known as Altyn Air when founded in 2001, it operated a small number of domestic and international services. In 2006, the carrier was rebranded as Kyrgyzstan Air before taking the name Air Kyrgyzstan in 2015. The company operated a mix of Soviet aircraft including Antonov AN24s, Yak 42s and Tupolev TU134/154s, with the latter often seen at Frankfurt before the airline was placed on the list of airlines banned from operating in the EU. The current fleet comprises the Boeing 737-300/500.

LAOS
Main gateway: Wattay International Airport – Vientiane

THOMAS INGENDORN

Lao Central Airlines, 2010–2014

When this first privately-owned airline was established in 2010 it was formed from the remains of Lao Capricorn Air Company and initially named Phongsavanh Airlines. It wasn't until 2012 that the name was changed to Lao Central to bring more awareness of the airline's roots to potential international customers. The Boeing 737-400 was the initial type operating flights both domestically and internationally, most notably Bangkok in Thailand. In 2013, the carrier received its first Sukhoi SSj Superjet 100, a type that was meant to eventually replace the ageing Boeings, as it had a further two on order. However, difficulties caused by political unrest in Thailand forced the suspension of international routes in late 2013, with remaining services the following year. There have been a number of suggestions as to the resumption of flights although none as yet have come to fruition.

LEBANON
Main gateway: Beirut Rafic Hariri International Airport – Beirut

Middle East Airlines (MEA), 1945–present

The flag carrier of the Lebanon, MEA is yet another post-war start-up with assistance from BOAC and, again, with the ever-present DC3 shortly after the initial type, the de Havilland Dragon Rapide, operated its first service between Beirut and Nicosia. Its early fleet choices seem to have been directly linked with whichever airline was a shareholder and offering its assistance at the time. During the BOAC era, the airline operated Vickers Viscounts and entered the jet age with the De Havilland Comet. In 1963, by which time Air France was its major shareholder, Sud Aviation Caravelles were acquired and later, Boeing 707s/720s and the

Vickers VC10. The Israeli raid on Beirut airport in 1968 saw the destruction of a number of these aircraft and stalled expansion plans. Restarting in 1969 with a Convair 990, the airline got back to increasing services and further extended its fleet when in 1970 it acquired the Boeing 747. Starting in 1993, the airline began a fleet renewal plan which saw them concentrating on Airbus types with the A310 first, followed by the A321 later in the decade and the A330 early in the new millennium. The airline's livery has been different forms of the ceder tree logo and red and green stripes since the early days.

TMA, 1953–2014

An all-cargo outfit, Trans Mediterranean Airways, to give it its full title, was originally founded in 1953 as both a cargo and passenger carrier. It wasn't until 1959 that it went all freight. Early aircraft were the Douglas DC4 and DC6A, in a mainly white livery. It wasn't until the arrival of its 707s that the all-green livery was applied. The Lebanese Civil War lasting from 1975 to 1990 took its toll on the airline's operations. A new livery consisting of green and yellow titles on a white and grey fuselage was introduced in 2002 as was a leased A310 due to the 707 being banned from Europe. Further pain occurred, however, in 2004 when safety concerns over these 707s caused the Lebanese CAA to remove the airline's AOC. This led to a six-year hiatus for the airline until 2010 when the airline re-emerged with a new aircraft type, the Airbus A300-600F, painted in a new bright blue and green livery This new incarnation only lasted until 2014, however, when all aircraft were returned to their lessors and operations ceased again.

MALCOLM NASON

Lost Airline Colours of Asia

MACAU
Main gateway: Macau International Airport – Taipa Island

THOMAS INGENDORN

Viva Macau, 2005–2010

Viva Macau was a low-cost airline set up in this former Portuguese colony under a sub-concession agreement with Air Macau. This allowed the new start-up to operate on the back of the Chinese-owned flag carrier. It was a similar structure to what was first pioneered in one of the island's main industries, gambling. This connection with the flag carrier did have its problems in that if Viva Macau wanted to send its 767-200s/300s to a new destination, it had to get approval from Air Macau first. However, it did manage to expand into quite a large part of Southeast Asia as well as Australia in addition to mainland China, and the two airlines were not in direct competition on any routes. The beginning of the end came in 2008 when, with the company struggling financially, the Macau government loaned the airline money aimed at giving the carrier some financial stability. Despite this, the airline had a problem with its fuel supplier which caused flight cancellations. This then brought the government back into the situation. Fearing the situation would harm Macau's image, it instigated the termination of the sub-concession contract which then enabled the Macau CAA to revoke the airline's AOC. Services stopped in 2010, and, despite appeals, the airline remains grounded.

MALAYSIA
Main gateway: Kuala Lumpur International Airport – Kuala Lumpur

Malaysia Airlines, 1947–present

Malaysia Airlines has had a number of names since its first commercial flight as Malayan Airways in 1947. The formation of Malaysia in 1963 caused the renaming to Malaysian Airways. Just three years later, another change, this time to Malaysia Singapore Airlines (MSA) signifying the airline becoming a bi-national entity with the newly formed Singapore. Malaysian Airline System was next just six years after that. Although the name never officially changed again, the

change in livery brought with it a modification in titles to Malaysia Airways which is how the airline is now known. The logo has changed almost as much, with the initial winged tiger giving way to one which includes the letters MSA, before moving on to various incarnations of the

Lost Airline Colours of Asia

current 'Moonkite' logo which has run alongside a livery incorporating red and blue lines on the fuselage. Throughout these branding changes the airline has expanded rapidly, utilising a huge variety of aircraft types, from the Bristol Britannia in the Malayan era through Fokker props and many of Boeing's jet offerings and even such oddities as the Scottish Aviation Twin Pioneer. Now the airline has a mainly Airbus fleet of A330s, A350s and A380s with the Boeing 737-800 for regional routes. Malaysia Airlines has had more than its fair share of tragedy with two infamous incidents involving the Boeing 777. Flight MH370 disappearing in March 2014 whilst on a service to Beijing, with its fate still not determined for sure. Just four months later, MH17 was mistakenly shot down by a surface-to-air missile over eastern Ukraine en route home from Amsterdam.

MALDIVES
Main gateway: Male International Airport – Hulhulé

PERRY HOPPE

Air Maldives, 1974–2000

This airline was the first National Airline of the Maldives, initially operating services domestically as well as to Colombo in what was then Ceylon with a couple of Convair CV440s interestingly named 'Flying Fish 1 and 2'. The company endured a rocky start with a takeover in 1976 and a cessation of all operations just a year later when the Maldivian government grounded its aircraft and froze its assets. By the early 1980s, the airline was back in the air flying purely to domestic destinations with a Shorts Skyvan. This aircraft was replaced later in the decade by a couple of Dornier DO228s.

International services were once again initiated during the 1990s when the company became a joint venture between the government and the majority shareholder in Malaysia Airlines. Destinations included Dubai, Trivandrum, Kuala Lumpur as well as the original, Colombo. The airline even made it as far as London and Paris in the latter part of the decade. These services being operated by the Airbus A300/A310.

At the turn of the millennium, the airline became bankrupt and ceased all operations although the finer points of this bankruptcy were never made public and where the fault lay is up for debate.

MONGOLIA
Main gateway: Chinggis Khaan International Airport – Ulan Bator

THOMAS INGENDORN

MIAT, 1956–present

Operations started with the rugged Antonov AN2 which must have been an experience for the Mongolian people first using these services. Given the airline was initially assisted by Aeroflot, the fleet remained based around Soviet types like the AN24/26, Ilyushin IL14 and Tupolev TU154 until they received their first Boeing 727 in 1993, thus meaning the airline was now able to operate internationally with its own aircraft. (The TU154 was wet leased.) The westernisation of its fleet continued into the decade with the arrival of an Airbus A310 in 1998 and the Boeing 737-800 after the turn of the century. This acquisition of more modern aircraft enabled the carrier to extend its international routes but at the same time ceasing all domestic services. In 2011, the airline received a new wide body to replace the A310, a Boeing 767-300ER, and by the end of the decade was operating an all-Boeing fleet to seven destinations, with plans to add more destinations and the 737 MAX and 787-9.

MYANMAR
Main gateway: Yangon International Airport – Yangon

Myanmar Airways International, 1993–present

The roots of the airline stretch back to 1946 when Union of Burma Airways was founded by the government in the years before the country gained its independence. Initially operating purely domestically, it was four years before the airline spread its wings internationally. It went through a couple of name changes: Burma Airways in 1972 and Myanmar Airways in 1989 when the country was renamed as such. Following all this, international services were subsequently transferred to Myanmar Airways International, set up in 1993. Previously operating a mixed fleet of Boeings, Fokkers and McDonnell Douglas types, 2001 saw a new corporate identity and following the government selling 80% of the airline to a private institution, the fleet started to be rebuilt around the Airbus A320/319 and began operating to destinations around Southeast Asia. Another rebrand occurred in 2019 with the arrival of its first A320 in September of that year.

NEPAL
Main gateway: Tribhuvan International Airport – Kathmandu

THOMAS INGENDORN

Royal Nepal Airlines, 1958–present

As with many start-up airlines, the first aircraft in Royal Nepal's fleet was the Douglas DC3, which, interestingly, many people in Nepal saw before they saw a car! The type of terrain in the country had a strong influence on some of the fleet choices, and over the coming decades the airline acquired the Antonov AN2, Pilatus PC6, Fokker F27, HS748 and de Havilland DHC6. In 1972, the carrier entered the jet age with the Boeing 727, reducing sector times to its regional destinations. Long-haul destinations became within reach when the airline received the first of two Boeing 757-200s in 1987. Aviation is important to the country with 80% of tourists arriving by air from destinations as far apart as Frankfurt, Singapore and India. The airline has struggled with corruption allegations either side of the turn of the millennium, with both airline and government officials either suspended or resigning. 2014 saw the arrival of a new livery and new aircraft types in the form of the Xian MA60 and Harbin Y12E. The latter to complement the Twin Otter but both exiting the fleet later, leaving the rugged Canadian twin prop still in service. The following year, the first Airbus A320 arrived, and the airline enjoyed a 20% increase in passenger numbers. Wide-body operations started in 2018 with the arrival of two A330-200s, whilst the remaining 757 left the fleet after 30 years of service.

MALCOLM NASON

Yeti Airlines, 1998–present

This carrier, whose claim to fame is that it was the first airline in South Asia to become carbon neutral, first started operations in 1998 with two de Havilland DHC-6 Twin Otters. These aircraft were later transferred to a subsidiary, Tara Air, which was set up to handle all STOL (Short Take Off and Landing) operations for the parent. Combined, these two airlines formed the second largest domestic airline in Nepal. International operations have been attempted in cooperation with foreign airlines. Having operated a number of aircraft for short spells over the years, the airline has now settled on the current fleet of the BAe Jetstream 41 and ATR 72-500.

NORTH KOREA
Main gateway: Pyongyang International Airport – Pyongyang

Air Koryo, 1955–present
Formed as a joint North Korean–Soviet organisation to operate services from Pyongyang to Moscow, it has only ever operated 'Iron Curtain' types, with many classic examples considered past their best still officially in the fleet today. Originally called Chosonminhang, up until 1975 it had still not entered the jet age, but this changed with the arrival of the Tupolev TU134/154 and later with the Ilyushin IL62 offering services to other Communist Bloc countries.

The end of the Cold War and subsequent shift in the political environment brought about great changes for the airline. Many of its international destinations were lost, and the airline decided to rebrand as Air Koryo in 1992 and acquired a Tupolev TU204 in an attempt to update the ageing fleet and provide an aircraft that could fly to Europe. Unfortunately, by then the airline had been placed on the list of air carriers banned on the continent due to persistent safety issues. China then became a source of expansion for the airline with new services to Dalian and Shanghai. 2010 saw the ability for European services but only with the TU204. However, all such routes were suspended and despite attempting services to Kuwait and Kuala Lumpur, the airline currently only operates to China and Russia in addition to domestic destinations. The livery has changed little over the years with the main change being the change of name.

OMAN
Main gateway: Muscat International Airport – Muscat

JOHN TAGGART

Oman Air, 1993–present

Oman was one of the partners in Gulf Air, but with others already leaving, Oman decided to start the process of setting up its own airline formed from Oman Aviation Services. Therefore, in 1993, a leased Boeing 737-300 took off from Muscat on a domestic service to Salalah with the first international service, to Dubai, four months later. More destinations followed in quick succession. The 737s were replaced after just two years with Airbus A320s, again wet leased. Over the coming years, routes were added and indeed lost and the airline stagnated somewhat. In 2007, the airline was recapitalised by the government and in doing so gained a majority stake. This also led to a complete pull out from Gulf Air and the commencement of its own long-haul services using the Airbus A310 initially to London Gatwick, then after two years the arrival of Airbus A330-200/300s helping it expand into more destinations. With these new aircraft came the livery we see today. Money seems to not be a stumbling block, as the fleet continues to grow despite never making a profit and now operates the Boeing 737-800/900 (plus hopefully the MAX) and 787-8/9 in addition to the A330s. It is in the process of retiring its Embraer E170s.

MALCOLM NASON

CargOman, 1977–1982

Very little is known about this operator and its single DC8-55. It mainly flew between Amsterdam and Muscat with a cargo of fresh food but could also be seen at other western European destinations like Frankfurt and London Heathrow. The airline/aircraft was purported to be owned by a Rhodesian air freight operator.

PAKISTAN
Main gateway: Islamabad International Airport – Islamabad

Pakistan International Airlines (PIA), 1950–present

Pakistan gained its independence in 1947 and it took just four years before the country formed its national airline with another three years passing before the first flight, using a Lockheed L-1049C Constellation. In it's early years, the airline also operated the DC3, Convair CV-240,

Vickers Viscount and the Fokker F27, the latter only being replaced in 2003 with the arrival of the ATR42, before moving into the jet age in 1960 with the arrival of the 707 and later the same decade, the Hawker Siddeley Trident. The 1970s saw the arrival of wide bodies with the DC10 in 1974 and the 747 in 1976. 2004 saw the delivery of the first 777 which

was to become the mainstay of today's long-haul fleet. Having operated the A310 from 1991 to 2006, the airline returned to the European manufacturer for its single-aisle fleet operating A320s from 2014, replacing the 737-300. The short-lived Pakistan Premier also operated with an Airbus, an A330-300 leased from Sri Lankan.

The airline's liveries have always incorporated the green of the country's flag, although there is a lot less of it now. Initially a green cheatline and an all-green tail with 'PIA' lasted until the 1980s when the green part of the cheatline was increased and had a gold line over the windows added. A few variants of this existed until 2004 when the main colours changed to a two-tone beige/white fuselage with a diagonal green band similar to the current livery but with a stylised Pakistani flag on the tail replaced by the current livery in 2010. A rebranding exercise in 2018 was to see a dramatic change with a markhor (a wild goat found in north and central Pakistan) in blue covering the tail, new titles and the flag placed by the aircraft's nose. However, this rather fetching livery did not find favour with either the public or the Supreme Court who barred PIA from replacing the flag on the tails of its aircraft.

Some 12 years earlier, in another move that drew a mixed response, the airline introduced four different regional tailfin liveries along with additional titles on the rear fuselage. There was one design for each of the country's four provinces and they were intended to replace the previous standard livery. This also failed to materialise completely, but all the liveries did

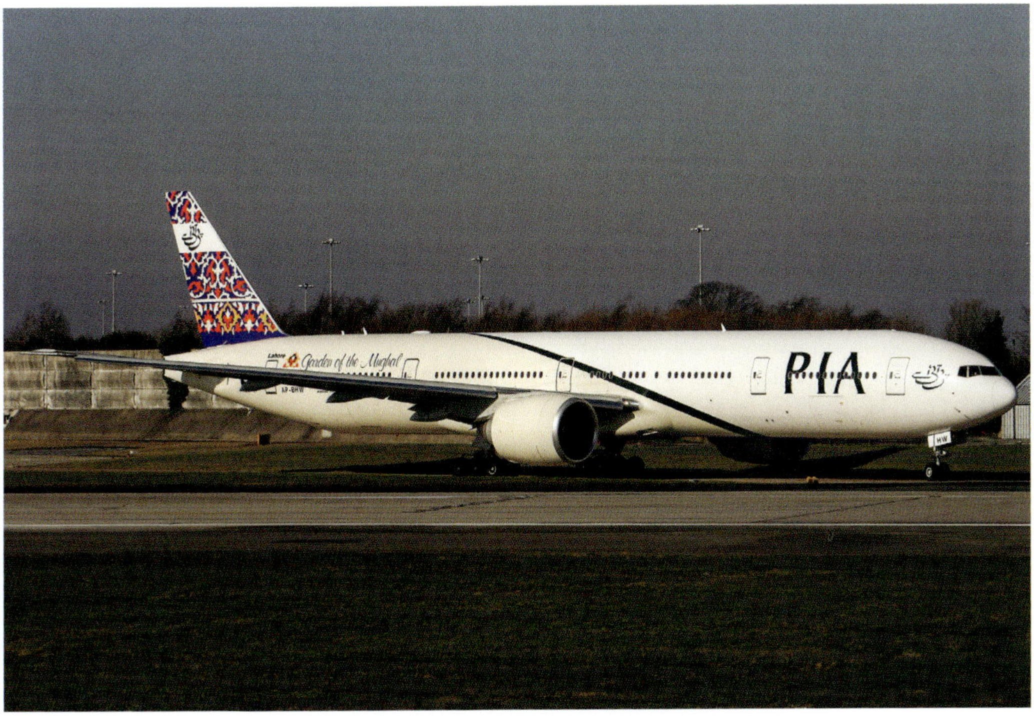
Lahore
Garden of the Mughal
AP-BHW
PIA

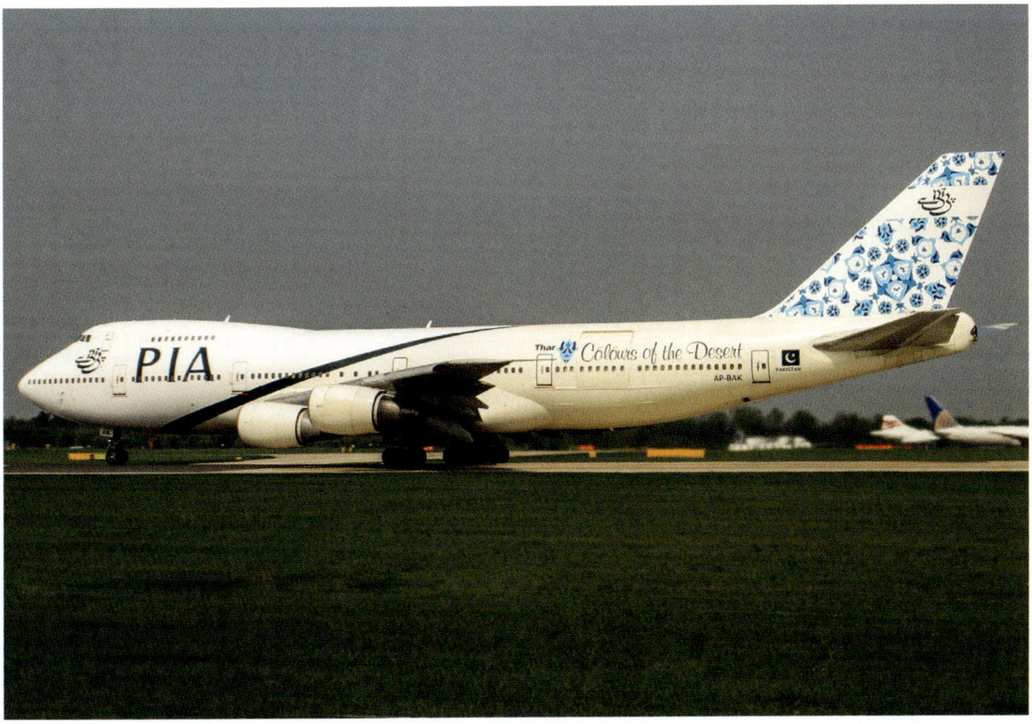
PIA
Thar
Colours of the Desert
AP-BAK
PAKISTAN

appear on at least one aircraft each.

The first to appear was inspired by Sindh province and featured a mainly blue design featuring the words 'Colours of the Desert'. The next was for the North West Frontier Province, sporting 'The City of Khyber Pass' titles on a mainly red and yellow design. Third was in the many colours of Baluchistan bearing 'Nature's Orchard'. Lastly, a mainly purple and gold design coming from the Punjab. It had 'Garden of the Mughal' titles. All aircraft were named after a city in the province as illustrated.

Shaheen Air, 1994–2018

This private Pakistani-based airline provided cargo, passenger and charter services in the region. Latterly also providing long-haul services to Leeds and Manchester in the UK. Initially operating Boeing 737-200s/400s, these were replaced with Airbus A319s/320s and also A330-200s/300s which were also used on the long-haul services. The airline's path was not a smooth one. In 2004 the airline was grounded by the CAA of Pakistan due to unpaid fees, only to be cleared to fly again just three days later after a payment was made towards these outstanding charges. It then went on to become the second largest airline in the country, but in 2018 passenger numbers declined in general, hitting the airline hard. It again found itself in arrears, and the Pakistani CAA this time declared the airline a financial defaulter and closed down all operations.

PHILIPPINES
Main gateway: Manila International Airport – Manila

Cebu Pacific, 1988–present

This is Asia's oldest LCC having been founded in 1988 as Cebu Air, becoming Cebu Pacific in 1996. Two years later, the airline temporarily suspended operations following a fatal accident on a flight from Manila to Mindanao. Initially operating a fleet of DC9s, 757-200s and A319s, it has replaced these starting in 2006 with an all-Airbus fleet, now comprising A320s/321s/330s of differing variants and engine options. However, domestic services are also to be operated by new ATR72-500s.

The airline's colour scheme was initially blue on a white fuselage, changing to the yellow and orange in 2006 but keeping the logo, a stylised bird's head, in the previous blue. In 2016, this livery received a revamp into what we see today, with the logo forming an integral part of the overall livery.

Lost Airline Colours of Asia

Philippine Airlines, 1941–present

The history of this airline stretches back to the early part of the Second World War when, in March 1941, the airline's first aircraft, a Beech 18, took off from Nielson airport in Makati, just outside the capital Manila. The war, of course, curtailed any great expansion, so it wasn't until 1946 that operations really began with a fleet of DC3s (which went on to serve until 1978!). Over the next few years expansion was rapid with services to Europe and over the Pacific to the USA using the bigger DC4 and DC6. 1962 saw the introduction of the airline's first jet, a DC8. Jet arrivals continued in 1966 but this time with another supplier in the form of the BAC 1-11. Returning to Douglas, it entered the wide-bodied era with the arrival of the DC10 in 1974. Boeing's 747 arriving six years later, the same year as the first-ever new aircraft, a Shorts SD360, acquired by the airline for its domestic services on which the current livery was first introduced. 1998 saw a low in the airline's history when it was forced to suspend operations due to the Asian financial crisis exacerbated by industrial action. This suspension lasted just a short period, and the airline went on to become profitable under two years later albeit at a much reduced size. It also was placed on the EU's blacklist of airlines, taking until 2013 before it was allowed back into airports within the EU. Approaching its 80th birthday, it currently operates a mainly Airbus fleet but sharing long-haul duties between the A350 and Boeing 777-300ER.

There have been considerable variations of the airline's livery, utilising forms of the twin triangle logo first introduced in 1960, replacing the 'PAL' in a winged oval used originally. The cheatlines of red, white and blue were finally removed when PAL went in the same direction as many others, introducing an all-white fuselage in 1970 along with the current sun-based logo.

QATAR
Main gateway: Hamad International Airport – Doha

Qatar Airways, 1994–present
Quite a 'new kid on the block' having started operations at the beginning of 1994 with two Airbus A310s quickly supplemented by Boeings 727 and 747, all of which wore the initial burgundy-based livery, which, as is often the case, is the predominant colour of the country's flag. However, in 1997 the airline received A300-600s on lease and with them, a new livery. The logo was still both on the tail and based around the oryx (the country's national animal), but it was now burgundy, with the rest of the aircraft being grey and white with Qatar Airways titles

also partially in burgundy. The airline has expanded considerably over the years and operated nearly every Airbus type produced and indeed has been the launch customer for many of the more contemporary models. Currently, it operates a mixed fleet of both Boeing and Airbus types, and although operated by the military, there is a Lockheed C17 painted in the current

livery which was introduced in 2006. The main changes being a larger logo and larger titles shortened to just say 'Qatar'.

There have been a number of special liveries in connection with numerous sponsorship deals entered into by the airline, from the 2006 Asian Games held in its capital city of Doha to its link with FC Barcelona.

SAUDI ARABIA
Main gateway: King Khalid International Airport – Riyadh

Saudia, 1945–present

The DC3 was again the aircraft of choice for this airline, although this time as a gift from the then US President, Franklin D Roosevelt, to King Abdul Aziz bin Saud. Initially called Saudi Arabian Airlines, the DC3s were supplemented by the Bristol 170. In 1962, jets arrived in the form of the Boeing 720; the airline became independent from government control just a year later. The airline's name was shortened to 'Saudia' in 1972 and with it the 'hockey stick'-type cheatline was replaced by the Saudi flag, dark green tail with House of Saud logo complemented by a cheatline of green and blues. Later in the decade, the Boeing 747 arrived and was deployed on the London route, with the Lockheed Tristar also being introduced. New routes all around the globe continued to be added throughout the following decades as were even more new aircraft types. These included their first Airbus – the A300, the Boeing 747SP followed by the 777

and over to McDonnell Douglas for the MD90 and MD11. In 1996, a new corporate identity was unveiled with the now familiar sand coloured fuselage and blue tail complete with revised House of Saud-style logo and the name reverting to Saudi Arabian Airlines. However, with a further rebranding exercise at the time of its Sky Team entry in 2012, this was changed back, yet again, to Saudia.

Flynas, 2007–present

It took until 2006 for another airline to get a licence from the Saudi government. Nas Air was formed as one of the country's first budget carriers, and operations started in February 2007. It was under this name that an order was placed for 20 aircraft in the A320 single-aisle family. However, having changed its name in 2013, it was as Flynas that the aircraft were delivered. Initially the airline served domestic and regional destinations but launched itself into long haul in 2014 when it became the first LCC to serve the UK market from Saudi Arabia. Initially serving London Gatwick and later Manchester with A330s leased from Hi Fly, the routes never became profitable (the first inbound service to Manchester had just six passengers) and were discontinued, along with most of its long-haul operations in October of the same year. In fact, Manchester only managed three months.

With the arrival of the airline's first A320neo in November 2018, Flynas made a slight revision to its livery, placing an 'f' on the tail and a slight modification to the tail colours.

SINGAPORE
Main gateway: Singapore Changi Airport – Singapore

Jett8, 2007–2012

This Singaporean cargo outfit had rather a short life, operating its first flight in 2007 from its home base of Singapore Changi to Hong Kong. Utilising two Boeing 747-200Fs, it also operated to Luxembourg, Amsterdam and Manchester in Europe, in addition to Asia. It targeted the cargo charter market so that it did not attract too much attention from Singapore Airlines' massive cargo operation. The difficulties began at the end of May 2011 when the airline initially failed to get its AOC renewed. In August of the same year, it finally managed to get its AOC back, but this was just for another year, and in 2012 the airline closed its doors for good with its aircraft languishing at Changi. Its livery remained the same throughout its whole existence.

Singapore Airlines, 1972–present

With the separation of Singapore from Malaysia in 1965, the brand new state was initially serviced by the joint state airline Malaysia–Singapore Airlines (MSA). However, with each country wanting to take the airline in different directions, MSA ceased operations and Singapore Airlines (SIA) was born. Given its desire to expand its international routes, the new entity kept the 707 and 737 of the former airline. New routes in Asia were inaugurated straight after incorporation, and the fleet was extended to include Boeing 727s, 747s and Douglas

DC10s. Services soon began to Europe, Australia and the USA and continued into the 1980s when SIA looked towards both Boeing, for the 777 and 747-400, and for the first time, Airbus adding the European manufacturer's A310, A300, A330 and A340, including the ultra long-range A340-500 which performed the longest non-stop flights at the time from Singapore to the US. SIA then went on to become the first airline to operate the A380 in 2007. The airline's livery has not changed too much since it shed the MSA livery at the time of incorporation. The initial livery had a blue and yellow cheatline with the silver kris bird logo on a blue tail. This livery was actually one of very few worn on a Concorde having been painted to one side of G-BOAD for three years. This was modified in 1988 by increasing the font size of the titles and the yellow rear fuselage being repainted gold. Two 747-400s were painted in a special tropical livery, but following a fatal crash of one of these in 2000, the other was immediately repainted.

SOUTH KOREA
Main gateway: Incheon International Airport – Seoul

Korean Air, 1962–present

Taking over from Korean National Airlines, which had been founded in 1946, Korean Air Lines, as it was then known, started operations in 1971 as a cargo airline, not commencing passenger services for another year until it started a service to Los Angeles. Early aircraft were Boeing 707s/720s, 727s and 747s, with McDonnell Douglas DC10s and Airbus A300s arriving a little later. In fact, Korean has operated a considerably varied fleet throughout its existence. These early types wore the first livery consisting of a blue cheatline and red tail markings including the initial Korean Air Lines logo of a bird inside a circle. Cargo aircraft wore a bare metal finish. It wasn't until 1984 that the now common blue and silver livery was introduced along with the taegeuk logo based on the concept of yin and yang, along with a name change to

Lost Airline Colours of Asia

Korean Air. The airline has had a rather difficult past with numerous fatal accidents leading it to be known as one of the world's most dangerous airlines. However, the last fatal incident was in 1997 with the airline now becoming a much safer organisation. Currently, it operates a diverse yet modern mixed Boeing/Airbus fleet right up to the Airbus A380, at least it did before the arrival of Covid-19!

Jeju Air, 2005–present

Formed in part by the Jeju Island's government with which it shares its name, Jeju Air was the first low-cost airline in Korea, created possibly to cash in on the fact that Seoul Gimpo to Jeju is the busiest air route in the world. It offers scheduled services within South Korea as well as other countries within the reach of its 737-800s. It is also a founding member of Value Alliance, the world's first pan-regional low-cost grouping. It currently has MAX 8 aircraft on order although time will tell if this is fulfilled. In the past it has operated the Dash 8 Q400.

SRI LANKA
Main gateway: Bandaranaike International Airport – Colombo

Sri Lankan Airlines, 1979–present

Following the closing down of Air Ceylon in 1978, the Sri Lankan government set up Air Lanka the following year, initially operating Boeing 707s leased from Singapore Airlines. Within four years these aircraft had been phased out with the introduction of Tristars, and leased 737s replaced by A320s. Following a partial privatisation with investment from the Emirates group in 1998, the airline was rebranded as Sri Lankan Airlines, and the red livery with the logo of a stylised bird called a Vimana was replaced by the current all-white fuselage and an even more stylised and flowing Vimana logo in red, orange and green. This livery is now found on the current all-Airbus fleet.

Lost Airline Colours of Asia

STATE OF PALESTINE
No airports currently in use.

MALCOLM NASON

Palestinian, 1997–present

Just like the State of Palestine, the country's airline has had to face many trials and tribulations over its short lifetime. Founded in 1995, its operations started two years later, albeit from Port Said in Egypt with Fokker 50s and Boeing 727s serving its close regional neighbours. However, in 1998 the airport at Gaza (later called Yasser Arafat International Airport) opened, and operations were moved into their homeland. In addition, an Ilyushin IL62 was introduced to help with route expansion. Unfortunately this was not to last that long, and in 2000, following increased tensions in the region, all services were grounded. Later, with bombing campaigns on the airport by Israeli forces, the airline, although back in the air, was forced to return to Egypt. The logistics of operating from a foreign country 30 miles away soon became a stumbling block. With tumbling passenger numbers, the 727 and IL62 were removed from the fleet before all operations were stopped in 2005. The carrier restarted in 2012 from El Arish in Egypt, but the same problems re-emerged, and just two years later operations were once again suspended. The plan is still to restart operations when possible, but at this point there is no stated timescale, and with the Gaza airport suffering more damage, it is difficult to see just how things might change for the better.

SYRIA
Main gateway: Damascus International Airport – Damascus

Syrian Air, 1946–present

After a short suspension shortly after operations began, Syrian Airlines restarted services with DC3s supplied by Pan Am who also supplied technical assistance to the airline in its formative years. A merger with Misrair of Egypt came about in 1958, following the uniting of Egypt and Syria forming the United Arab Republic and taking the name United Arab Airlines. The unity only lasted three and a half years, and when Syria declared itself a republic, a new airline was also born, this time with the name Syrian Arab Airlines and sporting a green livery similar to the original Syrian Airlines, although it fairly quickly changed to one with a blue and red cheatline. This incarnation took the airline into the jet age, receiving Caravelles in a slightly modified livery, doing away with the red.

In the 1970s, yet more political developments resulted in changes at the airline, with an ever-increasing view towards the Warsaw Pact countries, including operation of many Soviet types such as the IL76, TU154 and Yak 40. This time also saw another livery change with the first appearance of the mythical bird on a blue disc logo and titles of SyrianAir. Even with these closer ties to eastern Europe, it was to Boeing that the airline looked to for its fleet renewal, acquiring the 707/727 and 747SP which it operated through the difficult times of sanctions and declining passenger numbers of the 1980s. Recent fleet renewal plans have been more difficult, with US sanctions delaying the airline's A320s. Additionally, with the country mired in civil war, all destinations in the EU have been unavailable as has many parts of its own country.

TAIWAN
Main gateway: Taiwan Taoyuan International Airport – Taipei

China Airlines, 1959–present

This Taiwanese airline started out with just two PBY amphibians operating charters. However, it didn't take long for it to move into both scheduled and international services. Early jets operating these services were the Caravelle and 727. In 1970, the arrival of 707s enabled longer-haul services including over the Pacific and into the USA. Despite the loss of diplomatic relations with Japan stopping services there, the airline had, by the mid-1970s, acquired 747s including four SPs which could make the USA without the need for a stop. The airline continued to grow over the next two decades, introducing the 747-400, A300 and MD11. The initial blue-and-red stripe livery based on the national colours was replaced in 1995 with the 'plum blossom' (Taiwan's national flower) livery seen on new A330s/340s and 737-800s, right up to today's fleet which also now includes the 777-300ER and A350-900.

THOMAS INGENDORN

Lost Airline Colours of Asia

EVA Air, 1991–present

Not happy to sit on what was one of the largest shipping container companies in the world, Chang Yung Fa, the owner of Evergreen Marine Corporation decided that he would take to the skies also. Unable to use the name Evergreen due to the existence of the US-based airline of the same name, EVA Air was chosen instead. Initially, regional passenger destinations made up the route structure of the original 767-200ER fleet, but expansion was quick and the company soon expanded into the US and European markets, with the arrival of the 747-400. Domestically, the airline acquired shares in Makung Airlines, Great China Airlines and Taiwan Airways, merging them all under the Uni Air brand to become their domestic subsidiary.

After only four years, the airline was operating 20 aircraft and making a profit. With cargo already becoming a big part of its income through belly-hold usage, the airline started pure cargo operations in 1995 with an MD11 seen, by the end of the millennium, in Asia, Europe and the USA. Retired passenger 747s were converted into cargo use before settling on the current 777F.

At the turn of the century, the airline started a major fleet renewal programme, ordering the 300ER and 200LR versions of Boeing's 777 whilst also looking to Airbus for the first time, ordering its A330-200. 2005 saw the airlines team up to operate what was to become the hugely successful 'Hello Kitty' jets, with liveries on both these main types, attracting higher load factors.

The main livery has been similar over the years with an update in 2002 that increased the use of green to now cover the lower fuselage in addition to

Lost Airline Colours of Asia

a larger typeface. In 2015, a redesign did away with the orange trim on the tail and replaced the fuselage's green with a much darker, almost black colour, in a more flowing fashion which we see today on the Airbus A321, A330 and Boeing 777 and 787-9/10.

Mandarin Airlines, 1991–present

Although, in its current form, Mandarin is a domestic and regional airline, it started life with a service from Taipei to Sydney using Boeing 747SP and went on to operate a small number of others, including ones as far afield as Europe and Canada. It has always been majority owned by China Airlines although in differing amounts, and the parent merged Formosa Airlines into the Mandarin brand in 1999 whilst at the same time transferring the majority of international services to China Airlines, including all long-haul services like the one to Amsterdam where this MD11 was taken. Other aircraft operated by the airline in the past include Boeing 737-800 and 747-400, Fokker 50 and 100 as well as a very short stint with an A340-300.

The livery has not changed a great deal from the original design. The tail logo is the same, but the blue now flows down the rear fuselage where it is then accompanied by the lighter blue from the original cheatline.

Taiwan Airlines, 1991–1998 (Uni Air)

There is not a huge amount known about this airline; it was part owned by EVA Air and was merged into another EVA-owned airline, Uni Air, in 1998.

Uni Air, 1996–present

Formerly known as Makung Airlines, it was established to both serve the residents and to strengthen the development of the Penghu Islands region of Taiwan. EVA Air purchased the airline in 1996 and dispensed with this image as well as the name, to create Uni Air, aimed at serving a much wider customer base. In 1998, further expansion took place when the airline was merged with Great China Airlines and Taiwan Air whilst, at the same time, taking over the parent company's domestic routes. This restructuring created Taiwan's largest domestic operator with the airline branching out into the international market more recently. The original orange livery was dispensed with in 2012 when EVA Air announced a new corporate identity, which was also applied to its domestic subsidiary. Currently operating the Airbus A321 and ATR 72, Uni Air has previously operated the BAe 146, Bombardier Dash 8, McDonnell Douglas MD90 and even the Boeing 757.

TAJIKISTAN
Main gateway: Dushanbe International Airport – Dushanbe

THOMAS INGENDORN

Tajik Air, 1991–present

This airline's history can be traced back to 1930 and the creation of the Tajik air hub of the Central Asian air routes. Using YU-13s, it operated to many difficult-to-reach regions of the country. Heavily influenced by the then USSR, its aircraft choices reflected this influence, with types such as the Ilyushin IL14, IL18 and IL62 soon forming part of the fleet, with the Tupolev TU154, Yakovlev Yak 40, IL76 and the Antonov 26/28 following later. The Soviet Union also formed a large part of their international network. As has been the case with many airlines in the region, the break up of the Soviet Union saw a shift to a more westernised fleet of Boeing 737s/757s and 767s with just the AN28 remaining from its past. The carrier suspended operations in early 2019 but has since restarted on a greatly reduced scale.

THAILAND
Main gateway: Suvarnabhumi Airport – Bangkok

Asia Atlantic Airlines, 2013–2018
Established to focus on the Japanese market, this Thai-based airline operated from Bangkok's Suvarnabhumi Airport with Boeing 767-300ERs. At its launch, the airline's president outlined the company's big ambitions, alluded to in its name, with plans not only for Asia but over to Europe and across the Atlantic too. Unfortunately, these plans never came to fruition and despite a fleet renewal plan, the airline folded in 2018.

Business Air, 2009–2015
A relatively short-lived Thai airline, Business Air, was formed to take advantage of the booming tourism industry in Thailand and made its first flight in December 2009. The airline operated the Boeing 767-200/300 with the first HS-BIA, a 200 variant in a colourful blue and orange livery. Latterly, the 300s were in a more

sedate white but both having the same, almost butterfly-like, logo on the tail. Suffering from financial difficulties, the debts mounted up, leading to the Thai Department of Civil Aviation to order the airline to suspend operations in 2015. It received a brief reprieve shortly after, which led to a plan to rebrand as Intira Airlines with new ownership. However, this plan never made it to the air.

One-Two-Go, 2003–2010 (Orient Thai)

SPENCER BENNETT

SPENCER BENNETT

This Thai-based low-cost airline, operating a fleet of red and blue liveried McDonnell Douglas MD82s and Boeing 757s on domestic services, was based at Bangkok's secondary airport, Don Mueang. It is somewhat infamous due to a crash on approach to Phuket in 2007 where multiple flight crew errors, caused by systematic failures including corruption and lack of training at both the airline and the Thai CAA, were cited as the reasons for the accident. It was wholly owned by another Thai airline, Orient Thai, into which it was merged in 2010. Orient Thai itself folding in 2018.

Thai Airways International, 1960–present

The Thai flag carrier was established as a joint venture between the then Thai domestic airline, Thai Airways Company, and SAS with the intention of creating an international affiliate operating regional routes. This connection lasting for 17 years. In the 1970s and 1980s, the airline started to fly further afield with services to Europe, then Australia and latterly, the USA. At the end of the 1980s, both carriers were merged and, shortly after, it was privatised. In the run up to and during the early part of the new millennium, Thai was really busy. It (with SAS, Air Canada, Lufthansa and United Airlines) founded the Star Alliance. The Airbus A300s, Douglas DC8s, DC10s and Boeing 747s used on the intercontinental routes were starting to be replaced with the Boeing 777 and Airbus A330/340 amongst others; the previous livery was replaced with the current, very purple livery in a brand revamp, all whilst moving to their new home at Suvarnabhumi.

Lost Airline Colours of Asia

This time also saw the start of the airline's financial woes. In fact, fleet acquisition is said to be one of the issues leading to these financial difficulties, as the airline has operated an extraordinary list of types. The following decade saw the arrival of the A380 and the ordering of new generation types, the Boeing 787 and Airbus A350, and the launching of the low-cost subsidiary Thai Smile. However, there was also some downgrading of the airline's status with regard to safety and maintenance issues, although not enough for it to be denied access to any countries. It now operates a modern fleet of Airbus A330s/350s/380s and Boeing 747s/777s/787s.

NokScoot, 2015–2020

Formed as a joint venture between Singapore-based Scoot (itself a subsidiary of Singapore International SIA) and Thai-based Nok Air, this airline operated Boeing 777-200s from a base at Bangkok's Don Mueang to regional destinations in Asian countries such as Singapore, China and Japan. Having never posted a profit since starting, the carrier was forced out of business in 2020 as a result of the Covid-19 pandemic that caused so many others' ongoing difficulties. The airline's colourfully liveried 777s being returned to Scoot to await an uncertain fate.

TIMOR-LESTE (EAST TIMOR)
Main gateway: Presidente Nicolau Lobato International Airport – Dili

BN HISTORIANS COLLECTION

Transportes Aéreos de Timor (TAT), 1939–1975

TAT was founded when the country was a Portuguese colony and served destinations within that colony and its near neighbours. The carrier's first aircraft was the de Havilland Dove which went on to serve the airline right up until its demise. It also chartered aircraft as and when required to serve routes that the airline's Doves and Austers, and latterly the Britten Norman BN2A, could not. West Timor was served with a Merpati DC3 and Darwin, Australia with a Trans Australian F27 although this latter service was suspended in 1974 following Cyclone Tracy which seriously damaged the Australian city. However, the airline had much bigger problems just the following year when Indonesia invaded East Timor, forcing the airline's complete shut down.

JOHN M WHEATLEY

TURKEY
Main gateway: Istanbul Airport – Istanbul

Air ACT, 2004–present
Established in 2004 as ACT Airlines, this Turkish cargo operator runs its own scheduled and charter services in addition to ACMI (Aircraft, Crew, Maintenance and Insurance) services, initially with the Airbus A300F but now with Boeing 747-400Fs. In 2011, the HNA Group from China whose aviation affiliations include Hainan Airlines, Beijing Capital Airlines, Azul and Tianjin Airlines, to name just a few, bought just under half of the airline, with it rebranding as myCargo at the same time. The A300s had both titles on their fuselage, but the 747s had either an HNA-style livery, just myCargo/Magma titling or the livery of the airline they were operating for, such as Saudia Cargo, with small, additional 'Operated by ACT Airlines' titles. However, after six years, the partnership was dissolved with the airline reverting to being all-Turkish owned and again rebranding, this time as Air ACT and sporting a brand new livery, although the myCargo/Magma branding still exists.

Air Alfa, 1992–2001

Established to perform IT (inclusive tour) charter flights between western European destinations and its Turkish home, it quickly ran into difficulties, falling foul of a Turkish CAA regulation that required any airline to operate at least three aircraft. The following year, it restarted operations with a leased 737 running alongside its own 727s. A further year later, it added the A300B4 to the fleet to enable long-haul services to be undertaken. In 1996, the airline was modernised, with the fleet becoming all Airbus A320s/321s. At the turn of the century, the airline started to run into financial difficulties, and despite cost cutting measures, it folded in 2001 having only ever worn one, light turquoise-based, livery albeit with minor changes to the titles and cheatline. A brief attempt to resurrect the airline in 2002 lasted just a few months.

AtlasGlobal, 2001–2020

Originally called AtlasJet, this airline performed both scheduled and charter flights from its base in Istanbul, Turkey. The airline operated a number of different aircraft over the years from Bombardier CRJ700s/900s through to Boeing 737s/757s, Airbus A320s/319s and the MD83. Since the rebranding to AtlasGlobal in 2015, the airline operated an all-Airbus fleet of A321s/330s.

Difficulties began in 2019, when after initially suspending flights in November, they were reinstated a month later. However, after less than another month the airline suspended operations yet again and the A330s were returned to their lessor and parked at Shannon, with all operations halted two weeks later on February 12, 2020.

Turkuaz, 2006–2010

This Turkish charter operator flew its fleet of Airbus A321s/321s on behalf of a number of tour companies, mainly throughout northern Europe, until it was declared bankrupt in late 2010. This is the only livery its aircraft are known to have worn.

TURKMENISTAN
Main gateway: Ashgabat International Airport – Ashgabat

Turkmenistan Airlines, 1992–present
This flag carrier is in fact the only airline in Turkmenistan, and it operates domestic, international and cargo flights from its home base of Ashgabat. Its ex-Soviet era types from Yakovlev (Yak 40/42) and Tupolev (TU154) were phased out in 2001 to be replaced by an all-Boeing fleet, initially the 737 and 717, a situation that remains today with current types being the 737, 757 and 777, other than an IL76 used on cargo services. In fact, it was the first

ex-Soviet airline to operate the 737, and it has also operated the 767. Prior to the current green tail livery, the airline has had two blue-based designs. The airline has recently resumed services to EU countries after a ten-month suspension by the European Aviation Safety Agency.

Lost Airline Colours of Asia

UNITED ARAB EMIRATES (UAE)
Main gateways: Abu Dhabi International International Airport – Abu Dhabi
Dubai International Airport – Dubai

Etihad, 2003–present

Headquartered in Abu Dhabi, Etihad is the second largest carrier in the UAE and commenced operations in 2003 with a ceremonial flight to Al Ain, followed by commercial services to Beirut a week later. Previously, operations from Abu Dhabi had been operated by Gulf Air. The airline had big plans right from the beginning, announcing an order of up to 205 aircraft comprising a mix of firm orders, options and purchase rights at the 2008 Farnborough Air Show. At the time, this was the second largest commercial aircraft order in history. Just three years later, the first of a number of stakes in foreign airlines was announced, a 29% stake in Air Berlin followed up with 40% of Air Seychelles, 3% in Aer Lingus, 10% in Virgin Australia and 49% in Alitalia to name a few. The airline's money was also spent on a

number of high profile corporate sponsorships, potentially the most notable being the title sponsor for the Abu Dhabi F1 Grand Prix and main sponsor of Manchester City FC, both of which led to special liveries being applied to aircraft.

The cargo division was originally called Etihad Crystal Cargo but the 'Crystal' part was dropped in June 2012. The cargo division now just operates Boeing 777Fs but previously utilised A330-200Fs in addition to leased 747s from Atlas Air.

The main airline livery has only changed once since it first took to the skies but has remained the same colour palette despite losing the original tail logo.

Lost Airline Colours of Asia

UZBEKISTAN
Main gateway: Tashkent International Airport – Tashkent

Uzbekistan Airways, 1992–present

One of the many national airlines to come into existence following the dissolution of the Soviet Union in 1992. Taking over the Uzbekistan division of Aeroflot came with its aircraft, including the An24/26, Ilyushin IL62/76/86, TU154 and Yak 40. These early aircraft initially had slightly varying liveries based around blue and green cheatlines (when not in basic Aeroflot livery), some with a logo on the tail, others with just the Uzbek flag. Some also later acquired the livery still worn today by the current fleet. A year later, the airline acquired its first western-built aircraft, the Airbus A310, and then went on to order the Boeing 757 and 767. 1997 saw the BAe RJ85 also added to the fleet. It did not completely turn its back on eastern European manufacturers, becoming the launch customer for the Ilyushin IL114 which was assembled in the manufacturer's Tahkent factory. Since delivery, these aircraft have rarely operated more than what might be termed 'sporadically'. Currently, the airline operates a mixed Airbus/Boeing fleet with the most recent acquisitions being the 787-8 and A320neo.

Lost Airline Colours of Asia

VIETNAM
Main gateway: Tan Son Nhat International Airport – Ho Chi Min City

Air Mekong, 2010–2013
Operating a fleet of just four Bombardier CRJ900s leased from SkyWest Airlines, Air Mekong was a scheduled Vietnamese operator based at Phu Quoc, serving destinations throughout the country. Privately owned, it suspended operations in 2013 forced by heavy losses which the airline attributed, in part, to the CRJs' operating costs. The airline's intention was to restart once a more suitable aircraft was found, but after an extended period of inactivity its licence was revoked. There have been rumours of restarting operations over the following years but nothing as of yet is forthcoming.

Vietnam Airlines, 1956–present
From very small beginnings in 1956 as an arm of the Air Force, Vietnam Airlines had initial support from the Communist Bloc and operated the Lisunov Li-2 and Ilyushin IL14. Limited expansion occurred following the Vietnam War, including its first international destination, Beijing. Major changes came in the 1990s, as tensions with the US beginning to thaw a little, the airline started to receive western-built airliners of various types on lease from a number of sources, often on complicated arrangements to deal with the restrictions still in place by US authorities. Although still with a very varied and mixed East/

West-manufactured fleet, by the time the old, mainly white livery was changed to one similar to the current blue and gold, some rationalisation was starting with the fleet based around the ATR72, A320 and 767, with the 777 arriving in 2003. The arrival of the next decade saw a new share offering providing the funds to expand and renew the fleet, currently comprising the ATR72-500, Airbus A320/321/321neo and A350-900 with Boeing 787-9s/10s.

Lost Airline Colours of Asia

YEMEN
Main gateway: Sana'a International Airport – Sana'a

MALCOLM NASON

Alyemda, 1971–1996 (Yemenia)

The national airline of South Yemen was also known as Democratic Yemen Airlines and was founded by a presidential decree. Initially flying Douglas DC3s and DC6s to destinations in the Middle East and Africa, it very quickly entered the jet age with the arrival of Boeing 707s and 720s and by the end of the 1970s also had de Havilland Dash 7s. The 1980s saw continued expansion with the arrival of the Boeing 737-200 and a venture into Soviet types with the Tupolev TU154. Into the 1990s, and the airline both acquired its first wide body in the form of the Airbus A310 as well as even more new names, following the unification of North and South Yemen into one country. Initially Alyemda Air Yemen and later Alyemen Airlines of Yemen, at which time the fleet was an eclectic mix of Airbus, Boeing and Antonov, yet still with a DC6. Eventually, in 1996, the airline was merged with Yemenia to form a single national airline.

MALCOLM NASON

Lost Airline Colours of Asia

Yemenia, 1962–present

MALCOLM NASON

Although the roots of the airline could be traced back to the mid-1940s when Yemen Airlines was founded by the then King Ahmed bin Yahya, when the country was proclaimed as a republic in 1962, a new airline licence was issued which also made this "new" Yemen Airlines the country's flag carrier. A period of cooperation with United Arab Airlines ensued until 1972, when a reorganisation took place including a name change to Yemen Airways, with a further change to Yemenia in 1978 when a new airline was formed in conjunction with Saudi Arabia. By this time, the early Douglas DC3s and DC6s had been supplemented by Boeing 707, 727 and 737 jets with services being mainly regional but reaching as far as Rome. The 1990s brought more aircraft in the form of the de Havilland Dash 7 and Airbus A310, more routes as well as the merger with South Yemen's Alyemda following the reunification of the country.

Into the new millennium and the airline had increased its number of destinations and added larger aircraft in the form of the Airbus A330. Hard times were on the horizon though. Safety concerns, mainly due to alleged maintenance standards, caused the suspension of a number of routes, as did the suspension of the airworthiness certificates of two French-registered A310s. However, it was a worsening security situation within the country that eventually forced the suspension of all operations. Although services resumed for short periods during this time, the fleet is currently non-operational.